THE ART AND SCIENCE OF
EQUINE SHIATSU

A PRACTICAL GUIDE

Liz Eddy

THE ART AND SCIENCE OF
EQUINE SHIATSU

A PRACTICAL GUIDE

J.A. ALLEN

First published in 2023 by
J.A. Allen Ltd
Ramsbury, Marlborough
Wiltshire SN8 2HR
J.A. Allen is an imprint of The Crowood Press

enquiries@crowood.com

www.crowood.com

British Library Cataloguing-in-Publication Data
A catalogue record for this book is available from the British Library.

ISBN 978 0 7198 3505 6

Cover design by Sergey Tsvetkov

Typeset by Simon and Sons

Printed and bound in India by Parksons Graphics

Contents

Preface

Equine Shiatsu is a wonderful therapy, which unfortunately lacks the recognition it truly deserves. It is my hope that this book will help to change some of that. I fell into Equine Shiatsu by chance after being given Pamela Hannay's book *Touching Horses,* and became one of the first group of Pamela's students to graduate in the UK. It was never my intention to make a career out of Equine Shiatsu but to help other horses in the way I had managed to help my own. From there, people asked how they could learn and so began The Scottish School of Equine Shiatsu. It began as a simple introductory weekend, which is now the basis for this book, although much has changed and evolved over the last twenty years.

Having learned some of the basics, I was then asked for more and from that grew a course to professional level. This then spread from Scotland to France, Belgium, Italy and Finland and many of the Equine Shiatsu schools in those countries, are founded by former students. While teaching took up a great deal of my time, I have never stopped practicing. That is what really inspires me and even after twenty-six years since it all first began, it still amazes me and watching the change in the horses, seeing them develop a better relationship with their rider,

can be quite magical. Many of the horses that I work with today, look better and move better than they did over ten years ago. Some of them, I have worked on as competition horses and now as elderly ones. On occasion, there may have been too great an interval between sessions and they feel like they have become completely stuck, but because they have received regular Shiatsu, their bodies know how they should be, and after a few minutes, they can be transformed.

This book shows you how to give a basic Shiatsu from nose to tail for relaxation. It is just the start of your Equine Shiatsu journey but even complete beginners can have amazing results using the techniques in this book. But because we are dealing with an animal with a brain, and an opinion, of its own, I have tried to include suggestions to help when things are not going according to plan. Please always remember that each horse is an individual and so if things are not going to plan, change the way you are working. The horse is always completely honest and so if it's not working, you need to change. This can be on an emotional level or a physical one, and this book will explain how to do this too which can really improve your relationship with your horse.

However, the most important thing to remember is to *smile, breathe and enjoy.*

PART ONE

The Theory: The Science of Equine Shiatsu

CHAPTER 1

An Introduction to Equine Shiatsu

A Brief History of Equine Shiatsu

The principal pioneer of establishing Shiatsu with horses was Pamela Hannay from the USA, although the majority of her students came from the UK. She first came to the UK to teach in the mid 1990s, up until her untimely death in 2001. Pamela was the principal teacher of Shiatsu at the Ohashi Institute in New York and transferred her knowledge and skills to develop a therapy based on the techniques used in her human teaching.

Shi-atsu literally means 'finger pressure' but palms, fingers and elbows can all be used along with massage techniques and stretching. However, it is the form of Shiatsu used that allows it to work so well with horses. To explain this, we must go back to the beginning of Shiatsu as a therapy. While the origins of Shiatsu are thousands of years old, being an amalgamation of several types of pressure-point therapy and massage brought together and called Anma, Shiatsu was only formally recognised by the Japanese government in the 1950s. This was primarily the result of work done by Tokujiro Namikoshi. Namikoshi Shiatsu does not use the energetic channels and is much more physical and dynamic, working on areas of pain and neuromuscular points. His method requires sound knowledge of the musculoskeletal system, the nervous system and the endocrine system and therefore is more Western than oriental in its approach.

The use of the more traditional oriental framework was introduced by Shizuto Masunaga, who pioneered a more subtle and integrated form of Shiatsu, known also as Zen Shiatsu, where the giver and receiver converse through touch. This more supportive and gentler form of Shiatsu is what Pamela Hannay practised and brought to the equine world, although Ohashiatsu, as taught at the Ohashi Institute, uses methods from both Masunaga and Namikoshi. As such, every horse is an individual and every session will be different, depending on what the horse is happy to accept. Equine Shiatsu is considered to be a conversation with the horse; in essence it is something that is done *with* the horse, not *to* the horse and that is what makes it special, and what makes it work.

Zen Shiatsu

The general fundamentals of Zen Shiatsu apply to both equine and human practice but there are also differences due to the fact that we are dealing with a large animal. There are also other essential qualities, which are common to many different forms of oriental bodywork, that we can consider first.

Intent

A desire to help and support that is genuine allows the giver to free their own mind and thus be open to what is happening with the horse. It is often said that horses are mirrors and so if you are not truly engaged in the process then the horse will not be either. Indeed, being sincere in your wish to help can go a long way to make up for any technical inconsistencies in the beginner.

Breathing

The ability to breathe correctly enables so many more of the things that lead to a successful Shiatsu to take place. It means that you can relax, stay centred and it calms the mind, allowing you to stay in the moment and therefore feel more. The breath needs to be deep and steady, not shallow and disjointed. This is particularly important to remember if the horse becomes worried or upset about what you are doing, or what he thinks you might be about to do, because often at these moments we unconsciously stop breathing. As a mirror, your horse picks up on this and becomes even more stressed. Breathing out well is just as important, if not more so, as being able to breathe down into the abdomen. The feeling of filling the abdomen (or Hara, as it is known) gives a feeling of being strong and grounded while breathing out allows a feeling of release and letting go, which in turn aids relaxation.

Working with the horse to attain the best pace of work and amount of pressure.

Being in Hara

In oriental culture, Hara is seen as more than just the abdomen but has a spiritual aspect and indeed is regarded as the source of wisdom. It not only gives increased stamina and energy but also the ability to feel and to transmit Ki (energy/life force). To develop your Hara, the simplest ways are to practise breathing exercises and meditation. Western society promotes and praises the 'washboard' look and so, to hide the not-so-flat belly, many people change their posture, which in turn restricts their breathing and creates an environment where the upper body does most of the work. Bringing consciousness to the lower abdomen, allowing it to relax so that you can breathe correctly, helps the body to become one, move more freely and allow that feeling of power to fill the whole body, so that you can truly move from Hara.

Qi Gong, Tai Chi and Yoga, as well as many martial arts, are all methods which use the principles of moving from Hara and will also help develop Hara. Being in Hara creates a relaxation and calmness, which not only allows you to be more receptive to what you feel, but also makes working with the horse less tiring, as it is less physical because movement is not through muscular strength, but by moving from Hara.

Moving from Hara

Being able to move from Hara is key to allowing yourself to feel what is happening under your hands and to direct the appropriate amount of pressure at each moment. It comes from whole body movement, with lack of tension in the body. A more detailed description of how to achieve this can be found in Chapter 6, in the practical section of this book.

Two-Handed Connection

In Zen Shiatsu, there are always two hands on the body. One is quiet and still, known as mother hand, as it has a supporting role. The other hand is the working hand, which asks the questions of the body. Each time that you move this hand, you are saying to the horse, 'How do you feel about this?' Sometimes you will get a reply in the form of ears back, tail swish or alternatively sighing, chewing, eyes closing but the body itself will also respond to you. Do you sink in? Are you pushed way? Is it hot or cold? Learning to put these two together will take you a long way to developing the conversation with the horse that is Equine Shiatsu.

Simple Breathing Exercise

This can be done sitting or standing but the most important things are to be comfortable and be able to breathe. Place your hands lightly over your abdomen, just below your navel, and breathe normally. Do not try to change or force the breath but just allow it to happen. As you breathe in, bring your consciousness to your abdomen so that you can feel it expand as the air fills your lungs, and then feel it deflate as you breathe out. This is sometimes known as belly breathing. In reality, your lungs, when full, move against your diaphragm, causing the expansion of the abdomen. Do this for a few moments until it feels comfortable. Next imagine that you have a little ball of light, or a flame, in the middle of your abdomen and that every time you breathe inwards the light gets brighter and hotter so that the breath that you expel, which we can also call Ki, is brighter and more powerful.

Both hands need to be somewhere energetically significant, in this case on the same channel.

Care needs to be taken when considering the angle of pressure, as different stances, and different shapes of horse, can alter the angle at which you need to be. Consider the difference between a horse with a flat tabletop back to one with high withers and a prominent spine.

Shiatsu is one of the few therapies where the pressure is completely stationary. This can sometimes make it look as if nothing is happening but those long moments where you just wait and hold are often the most powerful. Be guided by your horse – he knows something is happening! If an area lacks enough Ki then you might find yourself sinking into a big hole; alternatively it may feel as if everything is stuck and you can't get in, and this might be where you need to use more 'moving' techniques such as massaging, percussion, rotations and stretches, such as are shown in the second half of this book.

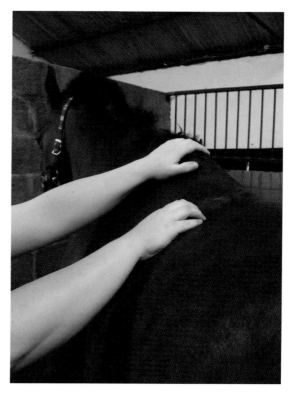

Working with both hands, showing the correct angle of pressure.

Perpendicular and Stationary Pressure

To be effective in your work, the pressure must be at 90 degrees to the body. This allows you to sink directly into the energy channel, which makes for a deeper connection with Ki. Horses are very energetically aware and will often shift a little to get you in the correct place. Alternatively, they may become restless and move if you have deviated from where you should be.

Working the Whole Channel

In Zen Shiatsu, the whole channel is worked to re-establish balance along its length. In human Shiatsu, it is common to work a channel two or three times but given the greater size of a horse, generally channels are worked only once by palm and once by fingers or thumb. However, there is no reason why you cannot work a portion of a channel more than once to ensure that there is balance. It is often talked about there being empty channels and full ones but the reality in Equine Shiatsu is that most channels that are out of balance have full areas and empty ones within their length.

Masunaga also developed an extended pathway of the channels so that those found in the arm (front leg) had a portion found in the leg (hind leg) and vice versa. However, working the primary channels in a horse usually takes as much time as the horse is willing to tolerate, and so knowledge of Masunaga's extensions on the horse are useful as a diagnostic tool, but are not so commonly worked.

A Horse Is Not a Human

When receiving Shiatsu, people will often become very relaxed and happy for the session to go on and on, but this is not the case with horses. If you go on too long, they get bored and it is possible to undo the good you may have done. It is preferable to do less and leave them wanting more than to do too much. A session should last about forty-five minutes give or take but more than an hour is usually too much.

The Difference between Acupuncture, Acupressure and Shiatsu

Around the same time as Pamela Hannay was developing her Equine Shiatsu, Amy Snow and Nancy Zidonis of the Tallgrass Institute were working on acupressure for horses. Acupressure and acupuncture both use traditional oriental theory at their base, but the aim and intention are different from Shiatsu. It also needs to be noted that there are different forms of acupuncture – Western and Eastern – but both can only be carried out on horses by a vet. The laws on this may be different in different countries but generally this is the case. The principles for acupuncture and acupressure are similar. Acupressure is useful for working on horses that are needle shy and also it does not need to be performed by a vet.

As one might expect, Eastern acupuncture uses the same oriental framework as Shiatsu but Western acupuncture does not. Rather, Western acupuncture makes a Western diagnosis and places the needles at or near that point. They may talk about the channels, often called meridians, but they have no real knowledge or understanding of them. It is possible to find vets that are qualified in the Eastern form but there are fewer of them. It is worth noting that many countries in the Far East have their own forms of acupuncture but here we will consider Chinese acupuncture as it is the most well known.

Table 1.1 Some differences between acupuncture/acupressure and Shiatsu.

Acupuncture/ acupressure	Shiatsu
Works on specific points called tsubos	Works on the whole channel including tsubos
Treats the symptoms	Tries to find the underlying cause
Uses herbs and lifestyle changes to aid needle or pressure work	Uses touch as one of the primary forms of diagnosis
Forms a treatment plan based on intellectually chosen points	More reliant on the individual giving the treatment and their quality of touch

Allowing the Body to Heal Itself

Behind many forms of complementary therapies is the idea that the giver is not doing the healing but allowing the receiver to heal themselves. In some forms of healing, the actual receiver is referred to as the healer because they are being helped to heal themselves. The question is, how does the body know how it should be?

There are two concepts to consider when looking at this. First, from the more simple and traditional side, the power of touch to comfort and restore is an instinctive thing to do, whether to hold a painful area or to give it a rub. If giving someone a hug when they feel low makes them feel better, then this shows how physical contact has the power to restore mental well-being as well as physical. Shiatsu is deeply relaxing although in the equine world some horses will fight showing this until they are alone as they do not want to show what might be construed as weakness. This usually occurs with mentally strong or dominant horses who have held pain for a long time. They have found their own way of dealing with it and to let go is hard. It is sad to say, but for some horses pain is normal. However, it is also said that only a relaxed body can heal itself. Using physical pressure and specific stretches to release tension and allow the body to let go both physically and mentally encourages the flow of Ki. When Ki flows well, the body is healthy and so aiding the free flow of Ki allows the body to be restored or simply maintained.

This simple version of things is how things have been explained for years but more is now understood about how the body works and what this really means in medical terminology. This will be covered in more detail in Chapter 2, but the second concept we should consider is that we can also say that Shiatsu turns on the parasympathetic nervous system.

The sympathetic nervous system is the fight or flight mechanism that controls the body's response to stress or danger. Hormones are released rapidly to increase heart rate, quicken the breathing and send extra blood to the muscles. It is involuntary and should be the body's quick energy boost to deal with stress. When the stress is gone, then the parasympathetic system should kick in and allow the heart and breathing rates to return to normal and the muscles to relax. It is sometimes known as the 'breed and feed' mechanism. However, sometimes through physical pain or discomfort, and sometimes through mental stress, people and horses find this difficult to do. Horses often have no choice about their job of work, their amount of rest or their diet, and if these are not correct, then there will be a build-up of stress. On top of this, owners may be aware when their horse has been injured or ill, but over time many animals, not just horses, suffer from repeated minor traumas. None of these things on their own are cause for concern, but added together they make things difficult and the end result is a stressed horse. Equine Shiatsu is particularly good at unwrapping the layers to allow a calm and comfortable horse to feel good about themselves.

Each Horses is an Individual

The Importance of 'It Depends'

While two horses may present with the same symptoms, that is no guarantee that the channels chosen, or indeed even the techniques used, will be the same. There may be some common ground because of the symptoms but the underlying cause will almost certainly be different; even if it is not then how each particular horse deals with their problem can vary. This is why the techniques used will vary from horse to horse. This is where Equine Shiatsu is an art for healing. Whether you are reading the horse's body language, feeling the Ki move under your hands or simply using your intuition to guide you, there are no rules or recipes in this part of the process.

Since this book covers basic techniques rather than specific channel work (apart from the Bladder channel), we can look at an example of two horses with neck pain. In both cases this shows up as an inability to stretch forward and bend correctly to both sides.

The first horse, Jack, has an old injury to his off-hind and so now does not use himself correctly. He is sound but in an effort to relieve the original pain he learned to subtly save the sore leg. He is now sound but nothing has told him that and this movement has become his default position. This creates a slight twist in the body, from one hind leg to the opposite front and up the neck, so the body zigzags in an effort to go straight until it gets to the head and it cannot go any further. As the neck issues are the final problem, rather than the initial one, it is necessary to balance the hindquarters, and release the shoulders, which will allow the back to stretch and aid the relaxation of the neck. Often in these situations a chiropractor or osteopath will work on atlas/axis or other cervical vertebrae but if the original area is not addressed the problem will return. In fact, Shiatsu works well with both these therapies as it can relax the muscles, tendons and ligaments, allowing any misalignments to be sorted out easily. However, it can also be the case that with good soft-tissue work and gentle stretches, the bony structures will realign themselves.

It is thought that the other horse, Daisy, had fallen over backwards and her behaviour became dangerous through pain. Her neck is very sensitive but so is her back and her pelvis on one side. She is also very suspicious and reactive, as she expects everything to hurt. In the first session, she needed lots of gentle holding and jiggling to try to establish trust and to help her let go. She was particularly worried about stretching anything. Small passive movement helps to unwind and also is not painful until Daisy is ready to let go. In the second session, Daisy has worked out that this Shiatsu is good, and is leaning in where she needs more pressure, stretching through her whole length. The greatest tension was initially held in the right-hand side of her pelvis and the right-hand-side upper cervical vertebrae but this time she knew what she wanted and needed. So sometimes when you believe that change will take a great deal of time, it does not. Every horse is an individual and behaves differently and therefore so must you. The ability to adapt to the needs of each horse, and to each part of the horse, is the art of good Equine Shiatsu.

Take Two Horses with Stomach Ulcers

Case Study 1

Milo is totally stressed, and permanently stabled, as he cannot cope with being outside. He has access to hay throughout day and night, is very sweet-natured to handle in the stable but his behaviour while ridden is getting to the point of dangerous sometimes and his owner is afraid. When he gets upset he then colics and this happens on a regular basis. The vet diagnosed stomach ulcers and he was treated appropriately. Everything would be fine for a while and then his behaviour would deteriorate once more.

With Shiatsu, the channels found to be most out of balance were Bladder, Stomach and Small Intestine. This certainly sounds very much digestive-system oriented but it was also found that Milo used one front leg differently from the other. One was quite loose to rotate and the other was locked solid. The Small Intestine channel runs over the neck, shoulder and down the front leg. Milo was also tight through this side of his back and was reluctant to use his abdominal muscles. It is true that a horse with ulcers will be reluctant to use his abdominals and stretch the back but so will a

(Continued)

15

horse who does not move easily through all four legs.

It transpired that several years before, Milo had been involved in an accident that hurt his shoulder and this was not completely resolved. When his work level got to a certain point, he could therefore not physically cope and his behaviour became violent, and then he colicked. In Shiatsu terms, we can explain that if he had been seen with Shiatsu after his accident then he would probably have presented with the same channels, but because things had been left for a long time, the imbalances in these channels had become so intense that the organs with which they were associated showed problems. If the original issue could be resolved, however, then so would the newer ones.

Case Study 2

Patch is a companion pony who has lived in the same herd for three years without incident. She is not ridden, is out at grass every day and is in a big communal barn with access to forage all night. She can occasionally be quite defensive with her near hind leg and can often be seen resting it. Out of the blue, she suffered four colics, with the time in between becoming shorter and her response to veterinary intervention becoming slower to resolve the situation. After the last colic, the owner suggested ulcers but the vets could not see that she would be a candidate for them. However,

scoping showed pyloric ulcers and she was treated appropriately.

With Shiatsu, the channels found to be most out of balance were Bladder, Stomach and Liver. She also showed an imbalance in the Lung channel. Patch is now back with the herd and her routine is exactly as it was before the colics started and no supplements, or anything to aid digestion, are needed.

This then is a more difficult situation to understand. We can offer up several hypotheses based on what we know and what was worked, but at the end of the day, they are just suggestions. However, if everything is resolved then that is all that matters. A possible explanation might be as follows: given her behaviour with her near hind, it might be reasonable to assume that there is some weakness and possible pain or discomfort in it. Among other things, the Liver channel is associated with tendons and ligaments. Patch has never shown any sign of lameness, or even being slightly unlevel, and is quite happy to gallop across the field to come in at night. However, there is a difference between one hind leg and the other. Since the Lung channel is associated with letting things go, it might be that there were some issues happening within the herd and, if she was feeling a weakness in the leg, these caused enough stress to cause colic and, subsequently, ulcers. It is something that we will probably never know, but it is said in Chinese medicine that the state of mind affects the state of body, and vice versa.

CHAPTER 2

How Shiatsu Works – Art or Science?

We have already mentioned how the intuitive and creative side is at the heart of good Shiatsu and the importance of the quality of touch in the giver. Various tools to help you improve this side of things will be discussed in later chapters.

But Shiatsu has a logical side that describes why what is happening is occurring, which helps to explain what is going on, why the horse behaves in a certain way and what might be the cause. In Chapter 3 we look at the Traditional Oriental Medicine side of this but as our understanding of how the body works increases, so much of this can be 'translated' into modern application.

The Art of Equine Shiatsu

The art of Equine Shiatsu is not unlike the art of riding. It concerns not only a technical ability to do what needs to be done but also a sensitivity to know when to insist a little more and when to back off. Is it that the horse will not do something or cannot do it? If it is the latter then more work must be done to enable the horse to do what is being asked of it. However, if it is the former then we need to ask, why does he not want to do it. Does he simply not understand? Is he worried that it might hurt? Does he have confidence in your ability to support him? The bottom line is

that we must always question ourselves first and not the horse. Equine Shiatsu will inspire trust between horse and human that will follow through into all areas of the horse's life.

From Fear to Zen

Deedee is a very sweet horse who had been abused and is the victim of some kind of bad accident, the truth of which is not really known. She now has a loving home but her owner was concerned that there were some issues that were still unresolved on a physical level, as well as having a general fear of everyone, except her owner.

During her first session she was very suspicious and jumped almost every time a hand was moved. She did enjoy the head work and relaxed nicely into that, but her stretches were not particularly enthusiastic and she was worried about standing on three legs. It also felt as if she was holding her breath all the time. Fast-forward to the second session a month later and she was

(Continued)

a completely transformed horse in terms of attitude. She engaged directly, leaned in where she needed more pressure, gave good stretches and completely let go. This meant that it was possible to identify the areas of greatest concern and also to address these much more specifically.

Of course, not all horses respond quite so dramatically so quickly but at the same time it is not unusual, and that is the magic of this therapy.

Quality of touch is key to Equine Shiatsu and being humble enough to accept that your horse knows his own body is a big part of making this work. Learning to let him take part in the conversation that is Shiatsu will benefit both giver and receiver. It can be the simplest of things that makes the difference. For instance, if you are working and the horse moves away, do not say 'stand still' but rather ask yourself, why is he moving away? If he is worried or concerned about an area where you are working, your touch may be too strong or too fast, so just slow down or even stop until he stops moving and start again. It is preferable, if possible, to keep at least one hand on the horse to maintain contact, but sometimes this is not achievable.

The Science of Equine Shiatsu

From Traditional Oriental Medicine to the Modern Day

For many thousands of years, the framework of Traditional Oriental Medicine has been used to diagnose and explain how imbalances have occurred within the body and how to restore them. Because there was not the kind of knowledge that is around today, this framework was taken from observation of the natural world and from what was happening within the body. As a result, the language used to describe this is often rather flowery and therefore dismissed by modern

science but, in reality, it was actually extremely accurate – especially considering that they would have no knowledge of the endocrine system and embryology, both of which can be used to 'translate' the language to something more science based. The traditional basis of oriental theory is covered in Chapter 3 but here we can look at something more up to date.

For many years, science has tried to prove the existence of Ki and meridians with varying degrees of success. In 1993, a study under C.K. Takeshige found evidence that something moved that was not at the same frequency as nerve pulse, or any other known substance within the body, but that is hardly substantial evidence for the sceptics. There has been countless research done on the effects of acupuncture but one of the drawbacks of these is that, in blind studies, often random points are used instead of specific ones; unfortunately it still means that needles are being inserted into the body and so these examples could still be classed as acupuncture.

Shiatsu is more difficult to use in a scientific study because everyone's touch is different and there can be no overall consistency. There have been evidence-based trials done in many countries; members of the Equine Shiatsu Association (tESA) in the UK followed one of the protocols used to carry out a study of the effect of Shiatsu on horses, which concluded favourably. In the past few years, there has been a great deal of research done into a part of the body that was generally ignored in the medical world, namely fascia. In 2015, fascial planes in horses were traced by Danish vet, Dr Vibeke Elbrønd and, quite simply, what were known as meridians are fascial planes.

One of the drawbacks in the interpretation of how Shiatsu works is the original translation of the Chinese by Europeans who visited China. The word 'meridian' is not an accurate translation but became so commonly adopted that, nowadays, even Chinese people will talk about meridians. However, the word 'channel' is now being promoted as a more accurate description. Dr Elbrønd's equine fascial planes are not exactly the same as a meridian/channel chart but, given the nature of fascia and that it is everywhere, there will be planes, or channels, everywhere.

Fascial Planes as Channels for Ki

Like fascia, a spider web connects and envelops. The raindrops are also an analogy to healthy fascia, which needs moisture to move. (Photo: Jean D on Unsplash)

Some cobwebs, like some types of fascia, are denser and as they dry out, they become less mobile. (Photo: Wolfgang Hasselmann on Unsplash)

What is Fascia?

Made up of collagen, elastin and ground substance, fascia, or connective tissue, comes in many shapes and forms but importantly it is found throughout the body, from the superficial layer under the skin to the deeper layers supporting the organs. It will vary in form depending on its role within the body but in all cases it is strong, flexible and gives structure. It both links and separates the structures within the body as well as allowing them to slide over each other within the body. In some areas it can store fat and water, and it forms a passageway for lymph, nerve and blood vessels. It forms a great web throughout the body that moves with the body. The key to healthy fascia is movement. In the words of Dr Gil Hedley, PhD, of *Fascia and Stretching: The Fuzz Speech*, 'movement melts fascia'.

When the fascia stops moving, it loses its flexibility, preventing one fascial plane to glide easily by another. Nerves can be restricted, causing a pain response, and it simply becomes more difficult to move. The less frequently an area of the body moves, the more the restrictions prevent it from moving. The build-up of fascial fibrosis, where the structures dry out and prevent movement between and within the fascial planes, can be caused by injury, lack of movement, overuse, inflammation or even incorrect posture. For horses, injury is often the cause – not only marked trauma but also subtle micro traumas through slips, bad saddles, bad riding and incidents where a horse may end up bruised, but not broken, and not given time and treatment to heal.

The problem of lack of movement is more likely to occur when the horse has a lameness or other problems where he literally cannot move. Unlike some people, horses do not generally become couch potatoes by choice. However, as a horse ages, he may develop arthritic changes that prevent him from moving as much or as easily as he would like; Equine Shiatsu is very helpful in aiding the horse to maintain his range of movement for longer, which in turn allows him to move, which aids healthy fascia. Indeed, many of the horses that I have worked with for years now look better in their twenties than they did in their teens.

Incorrect posture is, however, commonplace and is often mistaken for conformation issues. Often it is related to external influences and this will be covered in Chapter 4.

Does Ki Exist?

So, if the fascial planes are the channels where the Ki is said to flow, then what is Ki? Fascia is piezoelectric, which means that when squeezed or pressed it generates an electric charge. This charge runs freely along the plane or channel until something stops or slows it. This is one of the explanations as to why many acupuncture points are found around joints, a meeting place of structures where the 'charge' may meet resistance. The body is known to use electricity in other specific parts as well, such as the heart, muscles, brain and nerves. In fact, like Ki, it is everywhere.

In Chapter 1, the concept of the body's ability to self-heal was mentioned. This would suggest that Ki not only knows what to heal, but how to do it. The explanation for this comes from embryology. As an embryo develops from cells into a living being, there is organization to ensure that internal structures and organs are in the correct place and that head, legs and other parts of the body are where they should be. This requires something within the body to know what to do. If the body knows how to grow then it will also know how it should be and be able to repair. A more detailed explanation of this concept can be found in *The Spark in the Machine* by Dr Daniel Keown.

The Role of Hormones

The two main messaging systems of the body are the nervous system and the endocrine system. Some hormones are designed to rush in and out very quickly, but others take much longer to pass on their information. Even now, the role of some hormones in horses is not fully understood. The interesting point is that although people were unaware of such things as hormones in ancient times when Traditional Oriental Medicine was created, they were certainly very aware of their effects.

Let us take a look at two well-known hormones as examples, namely histamine and serotonin. Histamine is well known as the hormone of allergic reactions. It is supposed to defend the body against invading pathogens but sometimes it can overdo it and upset or irritate the whole body. The organ most associated with histamine is the liver, due to its role in breaking it down. In Chinese medicine terms, people and horses who have an imbalance in their Liver channel are often quick to anger and show irritability.

Serotonin is the hormone that creates feelings of well-being and happiness and most of it is produced in the gut. In Chinese medicine terms, the positive emotion that goes with the channels of the digestive system is comfort. In relation to serotonin's effect on the brain it is worth noting that this means comfort of the mind as well as the body. Balance in these channels will create that feel-good factor.

In the next chapter, we will look at this from a more traditional point of view but suffice to say that Equine Shiatsu does work, and it is possible to explain why in scientific terms.

The Holistic View

As modern scientific methods become more and more sophisticated, so the smallest of details and structures within the body can be examined, which has added greatly to what is possible in terms of veterinary and medical achievements. Thousands of years ago a more integrated view was taken. Everything is connected to everything else and also interdependent on everything else. This means that the body is looked at as a whole not only within itself but as part of its surroundings.

Observation – a Dying Art?

Without the diagnostic tools available to both doctors and vets nowadays, historic practitioners used their observational skills to understand which channels were out of balance. It may seem that this approach is not exact or accurate to us in modern times, but we still use it. For human beings, one of the techniques used is facial diagnosis, which includes looking at colours and lines on the face. On horses, this technique can only be used for one thing, which will be covered in the Observation section in Chapter 5.

Table 2.1 Observations from East and West.

Symptom	Western observation	Eastern interpretation	Correlation
Sneezing, pale face	Cold	Imbalance in the Lung channel	Respiratory system
Sneezing, red face	Allergy	Imbalance in a Fire channel	Immune system*
Dark bags under eyes	Tired	Imbalance in the Kidney channel	Ability to move

*In Zen Shiatsu

We may not rely solely on our observation to know what is going on within the body but we still make judgements based on our observations. Thousands of years ago, this was much more refined as it was one of the most important methods of diagnosis and so if some of the ideas sound far-fetched to us nowadays it does not mean they were wrong.

Physical Connections

When considering a problem or a disease that affects a particular area of the body, Shiatsu will look not only at the areas that are attached to that part but also its relationship with the whole body. Western medicine tends to concentrate only on the part that has the problem.

As we know more and more about the body, so treatments are tailored more specifically to that part but they often fail to take into consideration the knock-on effects. If we take navicular as an example, we know so much more than we did even forty or fifty years ago. Back then, navicular was thought to be a disease affecting the navicular bone, but now navicular is called a syndrome because we know that the problem may be related to bone, bursa or ligament and tendon. How many of these will be involved is now something that can be identified and treated accordingly. However, over a hundred years ago, navicular was thought to be a disease of the shoulder, and in many respects it is. A horse with hoof pain will try to take weight off the foot, which will cause tension in the shoulder. Not only that, the neck will become less able to move as it should, the back will tighten and the horse will also be unwilling or unable to propel himself forward from behind, and so this will also lead to tension in the hindquarters. Everything is connected to everything else.

Mental or Emotional Connections

It is said the state of mind affects the state of body and vice versa. Certainly if you are uncomfortable or in pain within yourself, you are unlikely to be the life and soul of the party. Whether it makes you miserable, angry or anything else depends very much on you as an individual. Likewise, if you are unhappy or angry with something then you can carry physical tension or move with incorrect posture, which in turn affects you physically.

With horses, things are slightly different. Personally, I believe that because horses are fight-or-flight animals, if they are physically well then mentally they can cope with most things; but if horses are in pain or discomfort then they may try to fight it and become aggressive, or run away from pain. Alternatively, they can shut down and become apparently lethargic and unwilling to move. Often matters are made worse by human behaviour when these 'problems' are sorted with stronger bits, tight martingales or the whip and spurs. Ultimately, a horse in pain or discomfort will change on a mental level too.

Some horses have learned to deal with their situation by not dealing with it. By this I mean that when asked to do something that they are worried about, it is almost as if they are holding their breath until it is over. Occasionally this state of mind becomes almost permanent and, as well as not letting go mentally and emotionally, they start to become unable to let go physically.

Lifestyle Connections

Unfortunately sometimes, the horse has little choice in these matters. The aspects of diet, being stabled or living out, being barefoot or shod, being clipped or not, which kind and size of saddle is used and what discipline they take part in is all decided by the owner. Of course, many horses live a good life and are well cared for, but sometimes the owner can be more focused on what they expect of the horse, rather than asking why things may not be going as well as they could.

We used to have a horse who absolutely adored to jump but dressage was apparently just boring and she would simply lose all impulsion and fall onto the forehand. I used to try to school her while out hacking but even then, too many leg yields from one side of the track to the other did not go down well. As for circles in the field, we would be about two-thirds of the way around and then she realised what it was and all impetus just vanished. The best dressage test I ever did was when the ring was right beside the show-jumping ring and both whistles went at once! I came to learn that because she was obedient we did not need to school her and so the occasional dressage test was tolerated because she knew she was going to jump afterwards. The moral of this story is that I could have made her school but she would have been bored, I would have been frustrated and then neither of us would have been happy.

If you can find a discipline that your horse enjoys and is good at, then they will give you so much more and it becomes a joy and a pleasure. Because the horse is more relaxed, this will keep his mental and physical wellbeing in balance more easily. In conclusion, it is necessary to consider all aspects of the horse's life to find the balance that is good health. Only when we look at the big picture can we find the cause, as it might not be immediately obvious.

Looking for the Cause Not the Effect

We have established that many different influences can affect why a body may be out of balance and that finding the underlying cause is key to where to begin to rebalance. Sometimes this is rather like peeling an onion, as different layers are revealed and need to be dealt with before the original source is found. This is particularly true when there has been a series of micro traumas, as each part that is protecting the one before it is discovered.

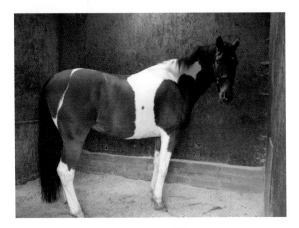

Smaller imperfections are more difficult to see.

Unfortunately for some horses, pain is normal and if they have learned to deal with the situation in a manner that they can cope with, then to remove that pain means change that they resist in case they can no longer cope. Sometimes, it can take a long time and progress seems very slow but at other times there can be a massive capitulation, in which case you need to give the horse enough time to process and accept things.

What we are looking for is where energy is lacking or deficient. This is the part that is not working and so something else has to work extra hard to compensate. If energy is deficient in one muscle group, then another one will become over-developed to cope. If, as a result of an old injury, a horse does not use one leg as much as the others, there will be tension. Over many years, this could result in damage and lameness in another leg but as the original injury has long since healed, only the lame leg is looked at.

So how do we find this? Simply, we ask the horse.

Talking Horse

If you have a situation as mentioned in the previous section, the only one who really knows where the pain comes from is the horse. Recent trauma will be painful and easy to find but, here too sometimes, the horse knows best.

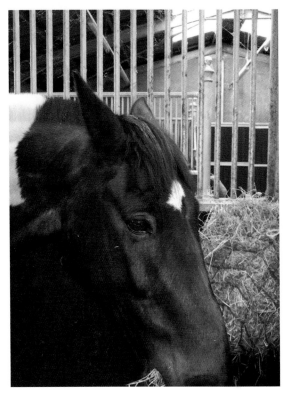

The horse knows where the pain is and can tell you.

While every horse is an individual with their own ideas about what is happening to them, there are breed characteristics in terms of how a horse behaves during a Shiatsu session.

Breed Characteristics in Responding to Equine Shiatsu

Generally, we can divide the different breeds into hot- and cold-blooded horses but there are some breeds of horse who need a category all of their own. This includes Irish Draughts and Welsh ponies of all size.

Breeds such as thoroughbreds, quarter horses and Arabs tend to be much more engaged right from the start, even if they have never had any Equine Shiatsu before; they work with you and can know what they want. Sometimes, especially with Arabs, they have already worked out that they need to stretch, and

Vegas's Story

When Vegas was purchased by his current owner, an old injury was noted in his near-side hock but it was judged that it would not bother him. He had, however, been out of work for some time after being a show horse. Initially he was quite tight in the head, neck and shoulders and was not really connected as a whole horse. Although he was quite spooky when out hacking, his ridden work in the school was going well until one day when asked for trot he was hopping lame. The vet prescribed an anti-inflammatory and ten days box rest but this made no difference.

I found him to be very tight in the lumbar area on both sides and unwilling to stretch back, but most noticeable was a hot, hard lump at the lumbar-thoracic junction on his dorsal spine, which, when touched, caused him to jump. Vegas improved very slowly but not enough and the decision was made to send him to the vet hospital. Here they found that nerve-blocking him just above the hock made a big improvement and there was some heat in the sacroiliac joint. Unfortunately while at the hospital, Vegas was becoming more and more violent with being touched around the near hock. Interestingly enough he never once showed any of this before, during and after with either me or his owner. The upshot was that he kicked and broke the MRI machine! He was sent home with advice to euthanise or claim loss of use.

With the consent of his owner, I decided to go back to the point where he had initially shown pain on his back and then if that did not help, we would look at the hock. It took time, with some setbacks as a result of fun in the field, but Vegas is now sound, being ridden regularly and enjoying life with lots of hacking out.

New painful areas that develop overnight should be worthy of note. However, if you have an area of chronic deficiency then often there is no apparent pain. It is as if the horse has decided to ignore that part of his body. When you find this, hold and breathe life into these zones, the reactions can vary from gratitude and pleasure, anger and confusion to completely ignoring you. The actual working of deficient areas is generally comforting but when working with horses it seems that the emotions or mental reactions to addressing these matters may not be so comforting. It is therefore important to allow the horse time to adjust and process what is happening. Never insist, and allow the horse to say no. This does not mean that you walk away but rather find a different approach. Go back to where the horse was happy with you working and begin again; try something different or work in a different way, faster, slower, more gently or sometimes more positively. Be guided by the horse because he knows his own body.

One of the issues that troubles people is knowing the difference between a horse saying 'I will not' and 'I cannot'. In the case of the former, you need to be creative and find a way to get the horse to do what you want by working differently, but if they physically cannot do what you are asking, ask for less. Any change, no matter how small, is progress and different horses need different lengths of time to realise that it is okay to accept change.

Dennis's Story

Dennis is a very handsome, and very tall, horse with beautiful natural paces but he fails to reach his true potential because of the tension held in his head, neck and shoulders. His history is unknown but his current owner has worked really hard to gain his trust and help him relax. He is now very happy with her but anyone new causes great stress and he is like a horse who is constantly holding his breath.

Usually when a horse has a sore area, they hide it away from you and present the other side, but Dennis did not do this. As I approached him, the head was as high as he could hold it and when I touched him on the shoulder, he flinched. In fact, as I moved each hand he flinched, but gradually he accepted touch and, while rather confused, tried to help. Working up to head and jaw work took time but he did accept some of it. In the next session he was happier to see me but still a bit tense and we managed more head and neck work. Unfortunately, between the second and third sessions, Dennis had got a fright when a bucket blew over while he was tied up and pulled back and so was very reluctant to let me up to the top of his head. I managed on one side, but not the other.

Before the fourth session, his owner told me she had spotted him doing his own jaw releases. She had watched him quickly raise his head and neck and tighten when he heard or saw something that he was unsure of, and then he seemed to notice this tension and could now work out how to release it. This was really good news. Often horses start to do their own stretches but this is more unusual, although not unheard of. It really did appear that Dennis had realised that Shiatsu was helping, as I managed to really get into his neck problems and after the session he just stood resting his head, almost touching the wall and letting it all soak in. This was a major breakthrough for a horse that carried so much tension. For horses who carry this much tension around the head, it can often take much longer for them to feel confident to let go as much as this.

when you ask for it, they go too far and too fast. This means that it might still hurt and the leg gets snatched back, so it is more important for them to do a smaller stretch and hold it long enough for them to be aware of how it feels. Their own natural extravagance of movement will allow them to use themselves as they should.

The opposite is true for natives, cobs and heavier breeds. For them, extravagant movement is too much like hard work and so every effort has to be made to show them that actually they can stretch, they can bend and they can use their abdominal muscles. Irish draughts are big powerful horses but if they do not have to do something, or it seems like too much

effort, they will take the easy way out. They therefore fall into this category too.

Welsh ponies are a law unto themselves. There are no grey areas. It is all black and white. Either they can, and will, do what you ask or they will refuse even before you have finished the question. On top of that, what was impossible yesterday may be the easiest thing in the world today and vice versa. This can be extremely wearing to work with but if you accept that it is what it is then the game becomes less fun and you will find a more cooperative horse.

While there are breed characteristics during a Shiatsu session, how the horse behaves immediately afterwards is a completely individual response.

A quick-thinking thoroughbred type.

A Clydesdale, who does little to help when lifting his legs.

How a Horse Behaves after Shiatsu

Generally, there are three common reactions to how a horse reacts immediately after his session and this is completely unique to each horse. There is no real way of knowing what will happen until after the first session.

Some horses want to sleep, some horses want to party and others wait two or three days until they realise they feel better. However, some of the sleepy ones do not acknowledge they feel better until they are alone, when they will lie down and go to sleep. If you have a 'sleeper' then you can ride the next day but if it feels as if you are on a lazy plod, do not ask for more; just sit there and be taken for a walk. On the other hand, if you have a 'party' animal who wants to show you how fabulous he feels and can now perform airs above ground, you may want to get off, wait twenty-four hours and try again. Many people like to give their horse a day off but it really depends on how much has been done and also what has been done. You will very quickly learn what is the best approach for your horse.

Relaxing and letting go, after his first Equine Shiatsu session.

CHAPTER 3

The Building Blocks of Equine Shiatsu

Although Shiatsu was not established as a therapy until the twentieth century and Equine Shiatsu first appeared in the 1990s, the theory is based firmly in Traditional Oriental Medicine using the concepts of Ki, Yin and Yang, and Five Element Theory. In Traditional Oriental Medicine, more commonly known as Traditional Chinese Medicine or TCM, which has been around for thousands of years, the understanding of how a body works was based on observation of the natural world. In the modern world, we know so much more but the original concepts of TCM still hold true in many ways.

What is Ki?

At its most simplistic explanation, Ki (Chi or Qi as it is known in Chinese) is life force or energy. Without Ki, there is no life. When you touch something that is living, you can recognise that fact and distinguish between that and an inanimate object. In Western medicine, this concept is not identified as such but it is still something that anyone can do without thinking.

Ki energy is not limited to living things but to everything in the universe, as everything is moving and transforming. Without the ability to move and transform, things become 'unhealthy'. If we take water as an example, a rushing fast-flowing river obviously moves but it also changes as white froth appears when it hits rocks. Here there is great energy. However, in a small pond there will be less energy, even though things are still moving through processes such as evaporation and water sinking into the earth. The pond may be replenished by rainwater or other streams and could overflow when full, and so there is a constant renewal to enable the pond to stay 'healthy'. Without this renewal of fresh energy, the pond will become stagnant and 'unhealthy'. One of the greatest forms of Ki is sunlight, given that sunlight and water are essential to life. Without Ki, or sufficient Ki, life will suffer and without good flow of Ki, things will cease to be able to move and transform.

There are many different types of Ki but for now, we can consider the three that can have the greatest impact on horses. First, as with people, there is Original Ki (sometimes known as Ancestral Ki), which is simply the genetics inherited from their parents. Strong genetic makeup will lead to a healthier, stronger constitution. The other two forms of Ki to look at are Air Ki and Food Ki, which will seem obvious in the air that is breathed in and the food that is eaten. Unlike human beings, horses are not always in charge of this aspect of their lives. also there is the chicken–and-egg matter of these two forms of Ki. In order to breathe well, a horse needs good lungs but to have good lungs, he needs fresh air. The same is true of the Stomach and Spleen channels for transforming and moving food into energy.

Why the Flow of Ki Is Important in the Body

As long as Ki is flowing smoothly within the body, good health is maintained. This balance is at the heart of a Shiatsu treatment and what the giver is trying to promote. Many things, physical and emotional, can disturb the flow of Ki and this will be discussed in detail in the next chapter.

Yin and Yang

From the concept that Ki is everywhere, Yin and Yang are used as a method to break this down into different qualities of Ki in order to identify what is happening within the body and how to approach it. Nothing is completely Yin or completely Yang and

that is why there is an area of white within the black and vice versa. There are equal amounts of black and white so they are opposing but also interconnected, still moving and transforming. As the energy moves, at different moments one or the other will become stronger, in the same manner of natural cycles such as the sun rising and falling and then the moon rising and falling. The movement created in this way provides balance but if one or the other becomes too strong or too weak then balance is lost.

Table 3.1 Qualities of Yin and Yang.

Yin	Yang
cold	hot
hard	soft
passive	active
weak	strong
introvert	extrovert
sinking	rising

It is also, as always, a concept of ever-changing degrees of Yin or Yang. There is no line over which, if something passes, it moves from one to the other; it is rather how something compares to everything else or to what was before. This is more easily explained by looking at some horses.

Identifying Yin and Yang Horses

Being able to identify your horse both physically and mentally as Yin or Yang is the first step to addressing the appropriate kind of touch.

The physically Yang horse is more solid, strong boned and well muscled. Generally speaking, this mainly includes native horses, cobs and draught horses but it has to be remembered that even some of these can be more Yin than others. This can be due to age (as elderly horses become more Yin as time passes), chronic illness or injury but also there are often horses of all breeds that are finer than others of the same breed.

Taijitu – the Yin Yang symbol.

The physically Yang horse requires deeper, more robust pressure.

The physically Yin Horse is fine skinned, has a more delicate bone structure and generally has larger spaces between its facial features (for example widely set-apart eyes) and legs. This typically includes breeds like thoroughbreds, some types of Arab, and Welsh mountain ponies. Many horses become Yin with age and injury as mentioned above.

The physically Yin horse requires lighter, more gentle pressure.

The mentally Yang horse is alert, playful and engaged. He is the kind of horse who gets bored easily and it is essential to keep up with him to keep him focused.

The mentally Yang horse requires quicker, more precise pressure.

The mentally Yin horse is quiet, reserved and even shut down or depressed. With this kind of

A bright, alert mentally Yang horse.

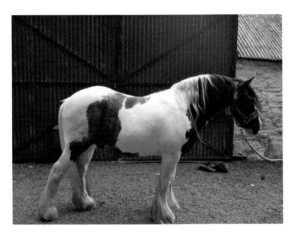

A strong, compact Yang horse.

A fine, delicate Yin horse.

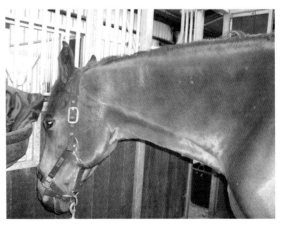

A quiet, more introverted mentally Yin horse.

horse, if you go too fast they will simply block you out and ignore you.

The mentally Yin horse requires slow, patient pressure (*note that the time required needs to be set by the horse and on occasion this can seem painfully slow until they learn to trust*).

However, not all horses fit nicely into the categories of chunky cob or fine thoroughbred and the subtleties of distinguishing where a particular horse will fit into these choices is key to getting your quality of touch correct. For example, if we compare Elvis and Ruby in the pictures below, then it should give more idea of what to look for.

Both of these horses have fine skin and coat, fine manes and tails, clean legs, large eyes and could not be classed as heavy in any way, but on a physical level, Elvis is more Yang than Ruby. He is bigger, more masculine, has a denser bone structure and smaller eyes. Mentally, however, Ruby is much more reactive and less tolerant. She is much quicker to show both pleasure and displeasure and to express it more. When Ruby's owner first contacted me, her initial question was 'Do you work with horses that kick?' Elvis, on the other hand, is more likely to say that he is not doing anything and plant his feet on the ground. He also falls asleep much quicker, as if doing something would actually require effort. When I first worked with him, his party trick was to

A **Yang Yang** horse requires deep, positive, quicker touch	A **Yang Yin** horse requires deep, positive, slower touch
A **Yin Yang** horse requires lighter, quicker touch	A **Yin Yin** horse requires lighter, slower touch

Assessing the horse, both physically and mentally, will help to decide how much pressure to use, and at what speed to work.

wait until one hind leg was picked up and then pick up the other one!

Lastly, we need to look at horses that are Yang at one end and Yin at the other. Most commonly, this is Yin behind and Yang in the front. This is when a horse does not use its hindquarters correctly and overloads the shoulders to pull itself along. Sometimes this is the result of injury but many

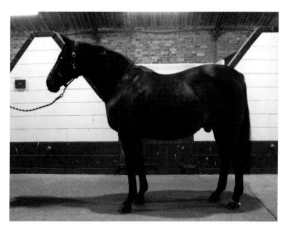

Elvis, more physically Yang, but more mentally Yin, than Ruby.

Ruby, more physically Yin, but more mentally Yang than Elvis.

Horse showing weaker Yin hindquarters, in this case due to sacroiliac strain some years before, leading to an overdeveloped Yang front end.

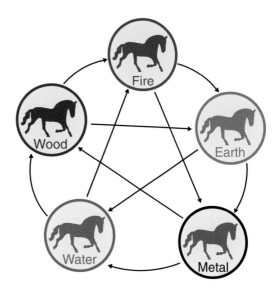

Five elements chart.

breeds of horse are actually designed to be more 'front-wheel drive' and have a natural tendency to pull themselves along, requiring less incentive to do so. This can happen from trivial injury, bad saddles or even bad riding. From the touch point of view, one must mix and match deeper and lighter pressure along with speed. To do this you need to be very observant of the horse, listen to what they say and react accordingly.

The Five Elements

The Five Elements represent further division of different forms of Yin and Yang and therefore Ki. The Five Elements – Water, Wood, Fire, Earth and Metal – are better described as the Five Phases or Five Transformations as this more accurately reflects the continual movement between them.

Identifying the Element in Horses

The biggest problem in comparing human theory to equine theory is that we have to consider different breeds of horse. The first thing to remember is that any breed can be any Element but some physical characteristics may create a tendency for certain types to be more likely to be in certain Elements. The next difficulty is that horses are not usually free to do what they want and human beings can create circumstances that radically alter a horse's basic Element.

Every horse and human is born with their basic Element. It determines their confirmation, whether they have big bones, a thick jaw, a long or short neck, the colour of their coat, and so on. Generally speaking, what a horse is physically is what they are emotionally but when we add in human interaction to this, it can change things and horses can find themselves moved into another Element. In extreme cases, it can be difficult to identify the basic Element if they have been stuck for many years.

Water Horse

Water is one of the more complex Elements in that it can take many forms. It can be anything between ice and steam, it can be a puddle, a gentle stream to a large waterfall or a tsunami. For this reason, Water horses can behave and react in many different ways.

31

Ticky – My Original Shiatsu Pony

The pony that I began my Equine Shiatsu journey with was frightened of everything but did not have an aggressive bone in her body. The fear and reluctance to go forward were very much Water qualities and indeed she could move well and jump well, if the notion took her. She was also very pretty, with great big eyes, and eventually wanted to please and be with you – most of the time – which are Fire qualities. She died aged twenty-four and, still today, I don't know if she was basically Fire that the Water had put out or genuinely a Water horse.

Physical Characteristics

Water horses flow. They have good bone structure and their movement is effortless. Indeed, often the best way to identify a Water horse is to watch it move. When you look at their bodies, this also gives the impression of flow as there are no definitions or breaks around the back of the shoulders or at the end of the ribs. The whole body just flows together creating an elegant horse. Generally speaking, they tend to be less fine than Fire horses and less strong looking than Wood horses.

Emotional Characteristics

True Water horses float through life unperturbed. Nothing is a bother. If they come up against an obstacle in their path, they do not worry about getting over or through it; they simply take the easy way out, choose the path of least resistance and either go around it or turn to go in a different direction. This makes them very amenable and easy to deal with. However, it is particularly rare to meet a true Water horse that is emotionally balanced.

The negative emotion that goes with Water is fear. This can range from mild apprehension to total terror and everything in between. It can be fleeting, such as when they first encounter something or someone new and are unsure at first, or it can become a way of life when something terrible has happened in their lives. In these circumstances, it is possible to reduce the imbalance that leads to this fear but it will probably always be there. It depends on what the original basic Element was beforehand, how bad the incident was and how life was before it happened. Unfortunately, a great many horses showing emotional Water characteristics are not Water horses but in a phase.

These horses can excel in any field with their ease of movement but it is their emotional state that is more commonly a problem. If shortcuts are taken in their training and things go wrong, they can get a fright if they have not understood what they were supposed to do. This leads to lack of trust at the very least and it can take a great deal of time and patience to restore it. Even after that, they can be easily stressed in situations where they feel under pressure and being able to have the freedom just to go makes them good endurance horses.

Wood Horse

When considering the Wood Element, think of a tree with its branches outspread upwards and out in all directions, its root system also spreading out in all directions, constantly growing and moving onwards and outwards. In this way, Wood people and horses are constantly looking and striving for more.

Physical characteristics

Wood horses are strong, well muscled, have natural tone even when not in work and are true athletes. They tend to be handsome rather that pretty or beautiful. Their movement is determined and purposeful. This makes them excellent competition horses.

A flowing Water horse.

A well-muscled Wood horse.

Emotional Characteristics

To go with their natural athletic ability, Wood horses are very self-confident and competitive.

They know where they are going and how to get there. They are creative and can get themselves out of trouble if things go wrong. They will push themselves to go that extra mile. This should make them easy to deal with and fun to compete but the negative emotion that goes with Wood is anger. When a Wood horse becomes frustrated, either because he is bored, he is not allowed to do things his way or he feels that he has been wrongly treated, he can become aggressive, which most commonly leads to faces with ears flat back, followed by flying hind legs. (In Equine Shiatsu it is useful to be able to identify the difference between an aggressive kick and a defensive one.) Because of their nature and good musculature, Wood horses are the ultimate competition horses. They love it and will go the extra mile. Unlike Fire horses (*see* next section), they do not need an audience to tell them that they are brilliant and so while they are good at dressage and show-jumping, they make great eventers. However, because they will push themselves, as they get older and more arthritic, which is not unusual after a life of competition, they will hide any weakness until they cannot go on.

Fire Horse

Fire is another complex Element. A 'balanced' fire is something that people congregate around and is a centrepiece but it can, sometimes for no apparent reason or with no warning, suddenly explode. The fire can also go out.

Physical Characteristics

Fire horses are beautiful. There is a delicate quality about them with lovely fine bone structure, large wide eyes, often with ears quite wide set and an open innocent expression. They are usually finer built than Water horses and their movement could be described more as dancing than flowing.

A beautiful Fire horse.

Emotional Characteristics

The positive emotions that go with the Fire Element are joy and love. A Fire horse is joyful, playful and loves to be loved and to love everyone else. As such, they adore attention and love to be the centre of it and to be admired; because they are beautiful, this comes quite naturally and so they get what they want. However, if the Fire explodes, and quite often this comes in the form of rearing (the Fire energy goes upwards but, unlike Wood, with no particular direction), then attention will be drawn to them and so this is still what they crave. The attribute of moving but without direction can also lead to horses that cannot stand still, and box-walking and weaving are both examples of situations where not only is the horse constantly moving but also is noticed. Alternatively, the Fire can go out. Often this is described as sadness but a more accurate way of putting it is lack of joy. These horses can seem depressed and unable to interact with the world around them. However, a

small amount of well-intentioned attention paid to them can easily start to improve the situation and their demeanour.

With their beauty and desire to be adored, these horses need an audience and so dressage, show-jumping and showing are all things a Fire horse will enjoy. Unlike with a Wood horse, however, the rider of a Fire horse must not expect total consistency. There will always be times when the Fire gets too much and so this makes them more difficult to accept for a competitive rider.

Earth Horse

From the earth, we grow plants to feed ourselves and our horses. It nourishes and is fruitful, so Earth energy is related to feeling safe and comfortable where our needs are met. The fruitful aspect of this is not only concerned with having food but also the ability to reproduce. In the Earth phase of the cycle, energy is beginning to descend and so the energy is quieter.

Physical Characteristics

Food is important to an Earth horse and so they have a tendency to easily become overweight. They are

A well-rounded Earth horse.

generally quite round and lack the natural muscle tone that an out-of-work Wood horse night have. Therefore the musculature is often a bit flabby. They can also be very grounded and movement may be slow or even non-existent.

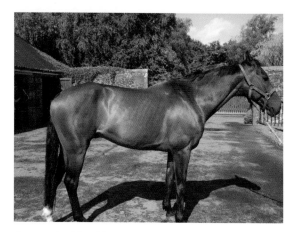

An angular Metal horse.

Emotional Characteristics

Earth horses like comfort and so that means not overdoing more than necessary. If this grounding becomes too much, it can be interpreted as stubborn. On the other side of the coin, there is a tendency to overthink things. This leads to worry and anxiety, which is dealt with by either overeating or becoming very fussy with food. If you are giving Shiatsu treatment to an Earth horse, it is a good idea to allow them access to a hay net. Some people believe that if the horse is eating then they will not have their full attention on what is happening but, for this type of horse, it is like removing a comfort blanket. Indeed if you get near to an area of discomfort, the eating will become faster and more frantic and this may be the only sign. Earth horses are not going to buck, rear and run off and so they make safe horses for novices or someone looking for a quiet life. They also make good brood mares.

Metal Horse

A metal box is something that we can hide behind or something that prevents us from moving on, and so metal is limiting. There are boundaries. However, metal is also a conductor and so one of the boundaries is where we take in and then let go. An inability to let go is damaging and many horses can be found in a Metal phase when it is not their true basic Element.

Physical Characteristics

Metal horses tend to look more angular than others of the same breed. This means that there are sharper

angles at the scapula, around the pelvis and even the angle at which the neck is held. They will not push themselves to go above and beyond as in their minds there is a limit to what they are able to do; if pushed beyond that point, they will simply refuse to do anything.

The Story of Peggy Sue

My daughter's first pony was a true Metal horse and had at one point been owned by a show-jumping family. She jumped well but had been pushed too far, so when we got her, we were told that she did not jump coloured fences. It took many years but she did get over this and would even jump little fences in the field on her own for fun.

It is fairly rare to find a true balanced Metal horse but there are a great many to be found in a Metal phase due to injury, old age, pain or being held down and contained by strong bits and martingales. In some of these cases, it may only show in one part of the body and by looking at the rest of the horse, it may be possible to ascertain its basic Element.

Emotional Characteristics

The most important point about Metal horses is that they are very polite. They like routine, rules and regulations and one of the rules is that it is impolite to bite and kick. For this reason their signals are much more subtle. If they are worried about something you are doing or are about to work on, look out for a twitch of an ear, a flick of the tail, a step aside. They can seem distant and introverted and, depending on the degree of this, reactions can vary from waiting patiently for you to engage with them, ignoring you completely, by not eating, to kicking out to keep you away. This is a defensive kick, keeping you back from being the boundary, which is different to an aggressive Wood kick and as such needs to be addressed in a different manner. While a shutdown Fire horse will respond reasonably quickly to some attention, a shutdown Metal horse is harder work to get a connection with, and if you do not get it right, the horse will simply block you out.

Well-balanced Metal horses make good all-rounders. They will do any discipline but not usually to the highest level. This may not matter because if the rider's level is less than that of the horse then both will be happy.

How the Elements Interact

There are two cycles within the Five Elements – the Cycle of Creation, where one phase moves naturally into the next (Shen cycle), and the Cycle of Control (Ko cycle), which helps to keep the energy within that Element in check.

Shen Cycle – the Cycle of Creation

Traditional oriental theory is taken from observing the natural world. In the Shen cycle, the characteristics of each Element and how they move from one to another can be likened to the seasons of the year, the story of life or even a fleeting moment when you move through the Elements so fast that you do not realise it has happened.

Moving through the Elements

Imagine the following example. You're out hacking, having a lovely time just walking along enjoying time with your horse (Water). Suddenly, out of nowhere a shotgun goes off nearby, giving you and your horse the fright of your lives (excess Water). Then you get angry (excess Wood), which very quickly becomes excess Fire as you imagine the terrible things that could have happened. However, you take a deep breath (replenishing Air Ki and therefore changing your energy) and realise that both you and your horse are safe (Earth). A moment later, you tell yourself that you did not do anything wrong, were obeying the rules, wearing a bright, easily seen jacket and had every right to be where you were (Metal). You try to go back to Water to enjoy the rest of your ride out. This is the whole Shen cycle but it may only have taken minutes.

Winter (Water energy) is still and quiet, ready to burst forth into spring (Wood energy) with its growing, exploring and creative energy; then summer (Fire energy) bursts into joyful, high colour and warmth; all these energies and Yang are expanding and rising. After summer, however, energy starts to descend and things begin to quieten into late summer (Earth energy), as fruits form and ripen until autumn (Metal energy), when they are ready to harvest. Things then settle back down into winter to reset for the following year.

As with the previous way of looking at the Shen cycle, so Water is the beginning and the end. A baby in the womb is waiting to be born and once birth has occurred, it starts to grow and explore its new world

(Wood) until it reaches adolescence (Fire), a time of few responsibilities but often a turmoil of emotions. As energy becomes more Yin, we move into our settled, nesting stage (Earth) until we can look back at our lives and reflect. However, as we move into old age we can also become limited in what we can, or want to do (Metal), either by illness or injury, or simply lack of energy, as we wait for death and the return of stillness (Water).

Ko Cycle – the Cycle of Control

This is the cycle of control and explains how each Element keeps another in balance. Water dampens down Fire, Fire melts Metal, Metal cuts down Wood, and Wood covers the Earth, breaking up its stability, and Earth dams up Water. The ability of each Element to gently limit another keeps everything in balance but if one of them fails to control another then imbalances occur. For example, if Metal does not control Wood, then Wood energy can become imbalanced. But what does this mean in real terms, or real equine terms?

Wood is a Yang energy and so is rising and expanding. As we have already noted, Wood energy is about growing and exploring and Metal is about containing and structuring. For this reason, a Wood horse that has no discipline and rules in its life will have no respect for anyone or anything and simply walk all over everyone. However, if there is too much Metal and this horse is contained too much, say by strong bits and gadgets, then he will either fight or lose his will to grow and explore.

How to Deal with Different Elements

Knowing the Element of a horse, both physically and emotionally, helps in understanding how to deal with them when things are not going smoothly, what discipline they might excel at and also to what injuries and illnesses they may be more prone. This last topic will be covered in more detail in the next section about the channels.

Generally, if the horse remains emotionally balanced then you can both be yourselves. If the horse becomes unbalanced and things start to go wrong, however, then you are the one that has to change in order to change the energy of the situation. Mostly we use the Ko cycle, the cycle of control.

- For a fearful Water horse, we can be comforting, reassuring Earth.
- For an angry Wood horse, we need to be cool Metal, polite but firm, while acknowledging that the horse is upset about something and adjusting the touch accordingly.
- For a playful Fire horse, we need to acknowledge the jokes. This is most important. For a Fire horse that is about to explode, we can be Water and just stay with them. wherever they move. However, there is always the possibility that we can become fearful and then we need to use the Shen cycle and become Earth, so that we pull the horse out of his Fire.
- For a stubborn Earth horse, we need to be strong Wood and use our muscular strength to pick up legs or be creative to get the horse to do what we want without them being aware that this might happen.
- For an introverted Metal horse, we need to be Fire and talk to them a lot so they find it difficult to ignore us and to praise any little cooperation to the skies. Everyone likes to be told that they are doing well and Metal horses are no different, but as they tend to do things well but not spectacularly, they may not get too much praise.

This may feel as if you are putting on an act, especially if being something you are not makes you feel uncomfortable, but with practice it really does work. Naturally, it is more difficult for people on the Earth/Metal side to be more Wood/Fire and vice versa.

We can also consider this when riding. All Elements of a rider can suit all Elements of a horse but some are better than others and it does all depend on the rider's ability to stay balanced within their Element; because we are only human, this is not guaranteed. The first thing we need to be is brutally honest with ourselves. We might like the idea of buying a super-competitive Wood horse but if we are Water and a bit scared or a bit Earth and not inclined to put the hours in, then maybe that is not the horse for us. An older, less-determined Wood horse might suit if we are happy to let them get on with their job.

Some combinations that work include:

- Wood horse and Wood rider – as long as they agree
- Earth horse and Water rider – the horse will look after the rider
- Metal horse and Earth, Metal or Water rider – a calm, non-confrontational horse is easy to handle

The possibilities are endless and it all depends on the nature of horse and rider.

Some combinations that do not work so well include:

- Fire horse and Wood rider – if the Wood rider gets angry or frustrated, it can all go horribly wrong
- Fire horse and Water rider – if the rider is balanced this will work well, but if they are frightened, it will not

- Water horse and Wood rider – if pushed too hard, this will not work and competitive Wood people like constancy, which is difficult to guarantee with Water or Fire

There is no such thing as a perfect combination but having an understanding of what Element you are and what your horse is can lead to a better understanding and therefore a better relationship.

The Channels

Having divided things into five with the Elements, it is possible to divide further into the energy channels. There are twelve paired channels with two in each Element, one Yin and one Yang, except for Fire, which has four. These are the primary channels but there are many more that are beyond the scope of this book. Ki flows everywhere through the body but, over the centuries, it was determined by touch and observation that Ki flows in a more concentrated form through these pathways. Each one is connected to the next and thus forms a continuous flow around the body.

In horses, there are two different interpretations of these channels. There is the equine one from ancient

The energy channels on the horse.

Colour Key	Yin or Yang	Channel
-------------------- - - - - - - - - - - -	Yang Yin	Bladder Kidney
-------------------- - - - - - - - - - - -	Yang Yin	Gall Bladder Liver
-------------------- --------------------	Yang Yin	Stomach Spleen
-------------------- - - - - - - - - - - -	Yang Yin	Triple Heater Heart Protector
-------------------- - - - - - - - - - - -	Yang Yin	Small Intestine Heart
-------------------- - - - - - - - - - - -	Yang Yin	Large Intestine Lung

times but more commonly used is the transpositional one, which uses the human channels transposed onto a horse. Given that there are considerable differences in the shape of a human and a horse, especially when looking at the neck and the shoulders, this accounts for the many variations found. Additionally, many of the channel diagrams are made for acupuncture where the location of points is important, but Shiatsu is designed to flow and so more simplistic channels are easier to work.

Location and Function

Each channel has a variety of functions and associations relating to imbalances, both physically and emotionally, but it is also important to remember that the channels also affect the area of the body through which they flow. Most of the channels are named after an organ but it is important to stress that an imbalance in the channel does not necessarily mean a problem with the organ. There are also two channels that are not named after organs but rather are a way of describing how the body was thought to work. First, Triple Heater refers to the torso, which is regarded as having three parts, Upper, Middle and Lower. Upper relates to respiration and circulation, Middle is for digestion and Lower is for elimination. Second, Heart Protector is seen relating to functions that modern medicine would equate with the heart, whereas in Shiatsu the heart is felt to be more to do with emotional stability.

In human Shiatsu, there are a great many functions that are not so much of a priority with horses, especially in terms of emotional imbalances. My theory is that because horses are fight-or-flight animals, if you can make them as physically able as possible, they are more able to deal with emotional problems. I also feel that horses have the same range of emotions that we do but I think it is very unwise to put a human interpretation on those emotions. Therefore, the table overleaf for function and physical imbalances is aimed at the equine situation. It should also be noted that this is only a very simple list

of the most commonly found associations. Finally, unlike people, it is the vet and only the vet who can make a diagnosis, and while sometimes relating a channel that is out of balance to a particular horse may give you an idea of what might be going on, it is only the vet who can say definitively.

It is worth noting that although the Stomach channel is associated with the digestive system, if the horse has an inappropriate diet then all systems of the body and therefore any channel can be found to be out of balance. Likewise, it needs to be explained that although a horse does not have a gall bladder, it still has a biliary system that performs the same functions, and if people have their gall bladders removed then they will still have a Gall Bladder channel.

Excess or Deficiency

How the channels are worked will depend on whether they are in excess, deficient or balanced. Then comes the matter of whether they are a little in excess or deficient or a lot, and this is why quality of touch is at the heart of a good Equine Shiatsu treatment.

Areas of excess can feel full, hot, swollen, sensitive or painful and as such are usually easier to find. Deficient areas can feel cold, empty, fragile and even lifeless but these are the important areas because they are where something is not working; the excess area is the compensation the body has created to deal with this. To make things more complicated, over time, areas that deal with long-term excess can in turn become stagnant and cold. In horses, because the channels are longer than on a human being, it is more common to find channels that have areas of excess, deficiency and balance throughout and these require a change of pace as well as a change of pressure as we tonify or disperse.

Dispersal and Tonification

Dispersal is usually easier for the beginner as they have a feeling of 'doing something'. With tonification, the opposite is true and it often looks as though

Table 3.2 Channel functions, primary associations and imbalances.

Element	Channel	Function	Association	Imbalance
Water	Bladder	Purification	Bones, back, spine	Back pain, poll tension
	Kidney	Growth	Joints, endocrine system	Arthritis, equine metabolic syndrome (EMS), pituitary pars intermedia dysfunction (PPID)
Wood	Gall Bladder	Distribution	Muscles	Muscle weakness, hip tension, PPSM
	Liver	Detoxification	Tendons, ligaments, detox	Weak tendons and ligaments, SI problems, laminitis
Fire (primary)	Small Intestine	Assimilation	Shoulders	Shoulder tension
	Heart	Emotional centre	Sweat	Depression, over-anxious
Fire (secondary)	Triple Heater	Protection	Head, neck, immune system	Atlas/axis problems, allergies, laminitis, skin problems
	Heart Protector	Circulation	Circulatory system	Laminitis, depression, skin problems
Earth	Stomach	Control of Food Ki, nurturing	Digestive system	Weak abdominal muscles, colic, ulcers
	Spleen	Transformation	Lymphatic system, transporting and transforming food	Stifle problems, colic, reproductive problems
Metal	Large intestine	Elimination	Digestive system, skin	Skin problems, jaw tension, headaches, breathing problems
	Lung	Control of Air Ki	Respiratory system, skin	Upper respiratory problems, dry skin, inability to let go

nothing much is happening except from the reaction of the horse who may really appreciate this work.

Most of the techniques in this book are dispersal ones as they are designed to get things to move – percussion, jiggling, moving skin and muscle, rotations and stretches. These are intended to move areas of Ki that are blocked or over-full, but in order to move them successfully so that they do not come back, we need to give them somewhere to go. For example, if you have a headache, you might hold or rub your sinuses, or just in front of your ears or the base of your skull, depending on where your headache can be found. When holding your preferred points your headache will lessen, but when you remove your hold, it returns. This is because in energetic terms you are preventing excess Ki from getting into your head when holding but you have not given it anywhere to go, and so it returns.

Tonification is opening and warming places that have shut down and lack Ki, and so gentle, patient touch is required. It is also vital to breathe properly to allow this to be as effective as it should but this will be addressed in the practical part of this book.

Restoring Balance

The aim of a Shiatsu session is to identify imbalances within the body and to work with them in such a way that balance, and therefore good health and well-being, is restored. In the next chapter we will look at how to spot imbalances and some of the causes.

CHAPTER 4

Recognising Imbalance in the Horse

The Balanced Horse

Finding a truly balanced horse is almost impossible, for no other reason than they are usually ridden by imbalanced riders. The truth is that what you have, so does the horse and what the horse has, so do you. That does not mean that we should not strive for excellence and one of the joys of Equine Shiatsu is when you have a horse that is at its peak, you can do some extra fine-tuning so that it can be even better. For horses at the top of their game, this can be the difference between winning and finishing in the top ten.

The Physically Well-Balanced Horse

The physically well-balanced horse will have:

- A leg at each corner
- Feet pointing forwards
- A bright, shining coat
- Carry the tail straight
- A mane falling to only one side
- Symmetry in the skull and skeleton
- Smooth, well-developed musculature
- Clear eyes and nose
- Normal droppings
- Good hooves
- A relaxed posture

The Mentally Well-Balanced Horse

The mentally well-balanced horse will be:

- Bright and alert
- Interested in his surroundings
- Calm
- Confident with strangers
- Relaxed

Causes of Imbalance in Horses

Channel imbalances can relate to function or location and in some cases both. In this last scenario, what happens is that over time something that started out as imbalance at the location of the channel becomes more deep seated, and other issues can appear. Some of the most common problems that an Equine Shiatsu practitioner will address are tight muscles and stiff joints. There will be imbalance within the channel that flows through this area, but there may also be imbalance in the channel that is

A bright and alert, but calm and mentally well-balanced horse.

inside. Therefore, imbalances in the Lung channel that appear as skin problems are more superficial than ones that show as breathing problems.

In some channels, musculoskeletal problems are more common than anything else and this is usually because, when or if things become more deep-seated, the problems are more likely to be in the remit of the veterinary surgeon. However, the exception to this is when the overarching imbalance is an emotional one.

External Factors

In Chapter 2, the concept of looking at all aspects of a horse's life was mentioned. Here we can look at these in more depth and the effect they might have on different channels. If there is an ongoing external factor, the result will be that no matter how much Shiatsu you give to the horse, the issue will not be truly resolved. Similarly, if you simply eliminate the external factor, the damage caused by it may not resolve itself automatically, and this is why everyone concerned with the horse's well-being should be part of a team.

Ill-Fitting Saddles and Bridles

This issue speaks for itself. Obviously, if a saddle is too narrow, too wide, moves forward or sideways, it is going to cause discomfort at the very least. In some cases, there will be actual damage to the musculature and any pain, and the memory of that pain, must be addressed. There is also the debate concerning treed or treeless saddles. Many people seem to be under the illusion that if there is no tree then there can be no damage, but this is not the case. An ill-fitting saddle is an ill-fitting saddle and it makes no difference if it is treed or not. What is important is that it is correctly fitted. Many countries are now fortunate enough to have properly trained saddle fitters.

Nosebands are the most common part of the bridle that cause issues. Anything that is too low or too tight can interfere with the horse's ability to breathe,

associated with the joints or tendons and ligaments. For example, if a horse has a problem with its stifle joint, there will be imbalance in the channels that flow through the stifle, namely Stomach and Spleen. Because the stifle is a very complicated joint, you might also find imbalance in the channel for tendons and ligaments, namely Liver, and the one for joints, which is Kidney. There may also be imbalance in the channels that flow through the muscles that support the stifle. Which of these we choose to work will vary from horse to horse, depending on what the actual problem is and how it manifests itself. This is where quality of touch is most important because we need to work on what we feel, and not what we think.

Sometimes the area that is affected can indicate how long a situation has been around for or how bad the situation has been. For example, the Lung channel is associated with both the skin and the respiratory system. Both are seen as a first-line defence for the body, the skin on the outside and the lungs on the prevent the normal movement required for swallowing, restrict room for the bit and even damage the nasal cartilage. If your horse puts his tongue over the bit or opens his mouth, there is a reason, and jamming the mouth shut will only cover it up.

Incorrect Biting

Biting is another somewhat contentious issue, with a choice of bits or bitless. In my opinion, it is what works for your horse that is important. While the choice and style of bit that is used is a matter for you, care needs to be taken in considering the size of the bit, the size and shape of the horse's mouth and the size of the tongue. For instance, if you have a horse with a narrow mouth and/or a big tongue then there is not so much room for a bit, and certain shapes and styles of bit will be better for this situation. Also, the actual shape of the mouth will make some types of bit more appropriate to fit into a flat, domed or arched palate. Once again, we are fortunate to have professional bit fitters to help with this.

Diet

The choice of equine feed currently available is vast and advice for particular situations is best sought from an equine nutritionist, so perhaps we can look at this more from a Shiatsu point of view. In Chapter 3, we mentioned Food Ki as one of the types of Ki to have the greatest impact on the horse's body. In simple terms, what this means is that correct feeding is essential for all functions of the body: growing, repairing, breathing, eliminating, keeping warm and providing energy. Without the correct balance of nutrients in the forms of fats, carbohydrates, proteins, vitamins and minerals, and water, the body is not able to function at its best.

Because every horse is different in terms of age, condition, amount of work and tendency to ailments, their reaction to food sensitivities can range from ulcers to laminitis. It is therefore vital to choose the correct diet for your horse. Incorrect diets can affect almost any organ in the body as it tries to deal with either insufficient nutrients or an excess of incorrect ones; as a result, the impact of poor diet can show up in any of the energetic channels.

Gadgets

There is a difference between gadgets and training aids. Unfortunately, the latter can have a tendency to become the former, whether this is because of the inexperience of the user or because someone is looking for a quick fix. Many types of devices used are supposed to encourage the horse to move from behind and stretch forward through the spine while staying soft through the back, neck and head. If your horse does not have any physical restrictions and is able to do all this, then the objective can be achieved. However, if your horse favours one side or one hind leg over the other, even to the point where it is not readily noticeable, then the horse will not move symmetrically and this will in time cause problems. If the horse is not comfortable then instead of relaxing into a comfortable position, they will fight it and lean or tense, which in turn causes more problems.

Unfortunately, this can happen even with something as simple as lunging. If your horse is not able to move evenly or bend correctly, then circles are especially difficult and so long-reining and encouragement of correct, equal movement in straight lines is preferable.

Hoof Care

Hoof quality, angles of the hoof and the state of the sole, frog and heels are the subject of much debate and, whether you follow the barefoot or the shod route, this is best left to the professionals. However, the old saying 'no hoof, no horse' is still very much true. As a horse owner, there are three things that we can control when it comes to our horse's feet:

1. What they eat – nutrition is a very large part of having good hoof quality.
2. Environment – horses are designed to move over a variety of surfaces in different weather conditions and so a stabled horse working mostly in the arena will not develop the ideal hoof quality. However, the opposite is also true: horses that live with constant wet in a muddy field will also not have optimum hoof quality.
3. Choice of farrier or podiatrist – some will be more experienced or more suited to the type of problems that your horse may have and it is essential to find someone in whom you have confidence.

Incorrect and uncomfortable feet will lead to many other potential problems throughout the body. We need to look at the legs as a series of building blocks where each bone and joint sits well upon the one below. If they do not, then pressure is put on the ligaments and tendons that connect and stabilise each part, which in turn leads to incorrect muscle development and movement.

Discipline

There are two different aspects to consider when looking at what discipline the horse is involved in. The first is the different pressures that particular disciplines put on the body on a physical level and the second is asking, 'Does the horse enjoy it?' We all put more into something that we enjoy and the horse is no different.

Different disciplines put different stresses on the horse's body depending on how they have to use themselves. At the top level, horses need to be more rounded in their approach in order to stay at the top of their game, but for the ordinary person having fun at whatever sport they enjoy, there is sometimes a lack of time to dedicate to things that perhaps they should. However, at an amateur level, some areas of horse sports tend to be harder on the horse than others and one of those is show-jumping. This is because show-jumping demands a lot of effort in turning, take-off and landing, all in a relatively small space for a matter of minutes. This can be very hard on the horse, especially if that horse is carrying physical discomfort or an external influence that makes things more difficult. Of course, this is true of any discipline and this is not in any way meant to be a detrimental comment about those who show-jump.

If you compete and travel to do so, then that too has an impact on your horse's health. Travelling in a trailer, or lorry, is hard work for the horse, on top of which being in an environment with unknown horses allows for the possible spread of infections. This may sound all rather negative but we have already covered the fact that some Elements of horse will thrive and really enjoy going to new places and competing. Once again, therefore, it depends on each individual horse.

Lifestyle

Some horses live inside 24/7 and some live out 24/7, but others will be in for part of the day and out for the rest of it, and this may vary with the seasons. Some may live in herds and others alone, or alone in an individual paddock. There are advantages and disadvantages to any system and, as always, it is not right to make judgement on someone else's choice

Jumping for joy, Patris Filius in his heyday (but see him aged twenty-eight in Chapter 11).

Some horses enjoy living out all day and all year.

Other horses are stabled part of the day, or year, or even all of the time.

may not be the most important thing, but more a realisation of how that choice of lifestyle impacts on the horse's body and what can be done to alleviate any potential problems.

As with people, sleep is very important for good health in the horse. If you observe a group of horses at rest, some will lie down and some will be standing. Standing sleep is not as deep because of the need to stand guard and so horses that either cannot lie down, or have no-one to guard over them, will not sleep as they should.

If a horse is stabled for long periods of time, being able to see other horses is also important. The relatively simple effort of allowing the horse to see not just out the door but between stables to the end of a block is good for well-being. However, being stabled too much also has a physical impact due to lack of movement. This will affect the whole of the musculoskeletal system and the digestive system, and care must be taken not to harm the respiratory system. Lack of movement can result in the horse not being able to keep warm, but of course we can rug them. Once again though, care must be taken to ensure that the rugs are not too heavy and cause pressure, by sheer weight, on the neck and shoulders. Everything that we do will have a consequence for the horse and it is our responsibility to make sure that it does not have a negative outcome for him. One of our biggest influences on the horse's physical and mental well-being, however, is how he is ridden.

The Rider

Simply put, what the horse has, you have and what you have, the horse has. If you put more weight on to one side then the horse has to carry this and will respond until he puts more weight on that side. But who is the chicken and who is the egg? If the horse puts more weight on one side, he will tilt you over so that in time you put more weight on that side too. We want our horses to be straight and symmetric but if we are not, how can they be?

based on what you feel is correct. There are horses that do not like being out in a field, whether with or without company, and there are also some who do not like being cooped up inside. How a horse is kept

An imbalanced rider will lead to an imbalanced horse, and vice versa.

If you are a one-horse owner, it is almost impossible to say who created the original imbalance, but if you ride several horses and they all have the same sort of problem area, then what, or rather who, is the common denominator? Interestingly, from a Shiatsu perspective, most horses who have owners that smoke have an imbalance in the Lung channel.

Looking at all these matters together, it becomes clear that there are so many things that influence and affect the whole picture, and when one of these issues is a major factor in a horse's life, it is easy to think that when you have resolved that, everything will be fine. The other situation that arises is when none of these things are a major problem and then it is assumed that everything is well. Unfortunately, many of the horses that I see do not have one factor that can be identified by the relevant professional but rather a collection of minor issues that add up to make an uncomfortable horse.

The next question is, therefore, 'Is an uncomfortable horse also an unhappy horse?' The topic of equine emotions, and whether an animal feels emotions or is just acting on instinct, is a widely debated one.

Look after Yourself to Look after Your Horse

One of my Equine Shiatsu students had what was deemed a lazy horse and was constantly being told to wear spurs or 'get after him with a stick'. Her gut instinct told her this was not the right approach. During the course, we cover an element of human Shiatsu and it was discovered that her sacroiliac joint was out of alignment and so we corrected it. When she next went out on her horse, he was flying. It was not the horse that had the problem but his rider as she blocked his forward movement. It is, unfortunately, a common occurrence in the horse world to spend lots of money on our horses when perhaps sometimes we should also look after ourselves.

Some months later she had a fall and noticed immediately that her horse had once again stopped going forward. A visit to a local therapist to check her out meant once again the horse was able to move freely. The moral of this story is not that we need to be in perfect balance to ride but that we need to be aware of our bodies and what we can do to help ourselves and, ultimately, our horses.

Emotional Aspects

Because Shiatsu works on all systems of the body, creating deep relaxation, in human beings it is known to help anxiety, depression and emotional stress. It therefore makes sense that any emotional imbalances in horses too will be relieved. However, we need to consider the general emotional responses of the horse. As mentioned previously, I believe that horses have the same range of emotions that people do but I think it is very important not to put a human interpretation on those emotions. I also think that because horses are fight-or-flight animals, if you can make them as physically well as possible then they are more easily able to deal with any emotional stress.

In Chapter 3, in The Five Elements section, we looked at the emotional responses to various different imbalances and what we might find in relation to these. However, these tend to be related to physical imbalances and there are situations that do not fit into this picture. The most common imbalance found is in the Lung channel, with horses with absolutely no physical symptoms relating to this channel. In order to explain this, we need to look at the function of the Lung channel.

The Lung Channel

As we learned earlier in this chapter, on a physical level, the Lung channel is associated with the respiratory system and also the skin. If the lungs are the first line of defence internally then the skin is the first line of defence externally. Physically, you breathe in, your lungs deal with it and you breathe out. On an emotional level, things happen, you deal with them and you move on, but if you do not deal with them, they remain a problem. It is therefore possible to suggest that some trauma or stress has happened in a horse's life but if it is a major trauma then usually there will be physical signs often in terms of irregular musculature development. So why should we find the Lung channel found in healthy horses?

Horses are herd animals so they make friends and alliances to develop relationships with both humans and other animals where they live. However, when a horse is sold and moves to a new home, all this changes overnight. For some Elements of horse, this can be very stressful but for others, they learn a sense of self-reliance and hold on to a part of themselves so they will not have to deal with that sort of thing again. If like many ponies, they change owners a lot as their riders grow out of them, this ability can lead to an imbalance in the Lung channel.

In some strong-minded horses, you can also find imbalance in the Lung channel when they have learned to protect themselves from pain following an injury. They have changed their way of going to minimise the pain or discomfort of the original injury and have carried on like this, in many cases, for years. It may still cause discomfort but it is at a level with which they feel they can cope. When there is an attempt to alleviate that discomfort, they refuse to let go because for them that pain is normal and they worry that the alternative could be worse. In these situations, you can see and feel the physical improvements but the horse is reluctant to embrace the changes and it becomes necessary to address any imbalance found in the Lung channel to help them let go.

Anxiety and Depression

Anxiety can be caused by all number of situations and is often related to external factors, but something that can be helped is an anxiety which is caused by physical weakness. In these situations, all manner of behavioural improvements can be noted, from being calmer to ride to better with the farrier. Sometimes the existence of long-term anxiety can lead to depression where the horse stops interacting with people or even with other horses. This is more difficult to help but certainly not impossible. However, before embarking on a venture like this, it is worth considering how the horse moves through the Shen Cycle (the cycle of creation) and at some point will move through the Wood Element with its negative emotion of anger. Very occasionally, a horse that has been shut down discovers that it feels well enough and confident enough to express that anger. It is not personal and if you can help them through it, you can move on to the Fire Element and promote some joy.

Stereotypic Behaviour

Stereotypic behaviour was once listed simply as stable vices and includes cribbing, weaving, wind-sucking and box-walking. For many years, these behaviours were put down to external factors including boredom, social isolation and feeding practices. Indeed, all these play a part in such behaviours but it needs to be recognised that it is a survival mechanism as the horse attempts to cope with his situation. In TCM, the neck is seen as the link between the legs and the head/brain. The brain sends a signal and the legs move, but in horses that crib and weave, this message is interrupted by the up-and-down movement of the neck for cribbing and the side-to-side movement in weaving, causing the legs to also move in an unnatural manner. So can this signal be interrupted and corrected?

The short answer is perhaps, sometimes. Can the behaviour be lessened? Yes, it can. Identifying and removing the triggers that set off these behaviours are paramount so that management changes in relation to feeding routines and turnout can reduce any stress. Because these horses show stress-related behaviours, any reduction in hormones that induce a stress response and an increase in those that help restore calm will have a positive outcome. Since Equine Shiatsu does just that it can have a positive effect on cribbing, weaving and wind-sucking. It is worth noting that these behaviours are also a habit and, under stress, they can return; however, they can definitely be reduced.

Equine Shiatsu is a magical and very effective therapy and it is truly holistic. This means that we have to look at the whole situation in terms of lifestyle and external circumstances but also that it can benefit the physical and emotional or behavioural state of the horse. Taking all of these factors into consideration helps us to hone the skills needed to help make an oriental diagnosis, and find out where the imbalances that need to be corrected can be found.

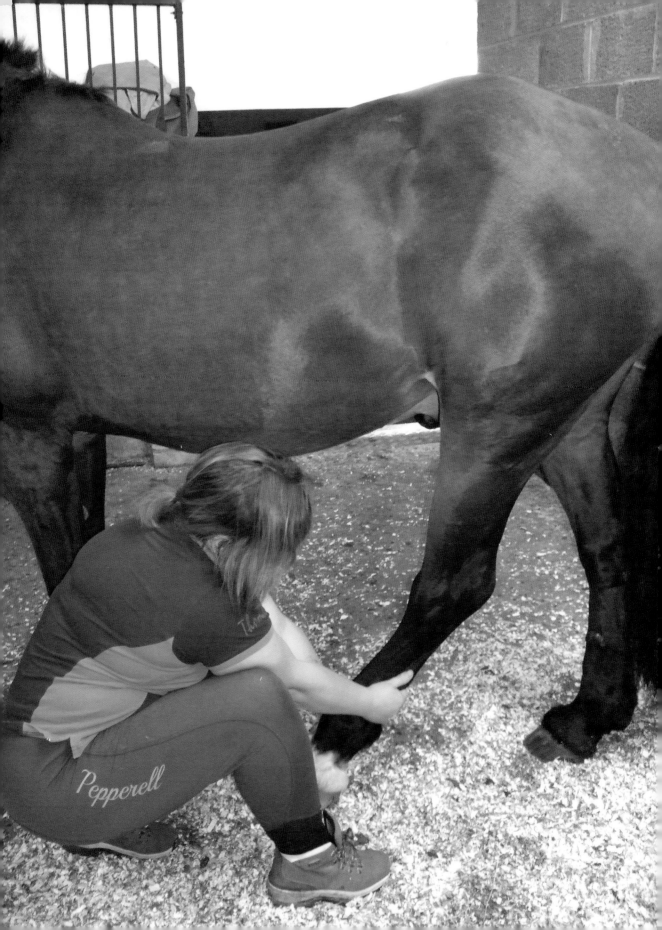

PART TWO

The Practice: The Art of Equine Shiatsu

CHAPTER 5

The Cornerstones of Oriental Diagnosis

There are four cornerstones in oriental diagnosis, but in relation to the horse there are really only two. The other two cornerstones can sometimes be used but not as much as in human diagnosis.

The four cornerstones are:

- Asking questions
- Listening and smelling
- Observation
- Touch

Asking Questions

We cannot ask questions directly of the horse but we can ask the owner and the vet. However, these sometimes have drawbacks as the owner may not know the full or true history of the horse. Also, while the owner may give you what they believe to be true, sometimes it is not. Many years ago I went to see a horse who the owner said was very nervous. I quickly saw that the nervous one was not the horse!

If you have a situation where there has been a problem and it is not resolved, in spite of all veterinary intervention, then it is interesting to know what the vets thought it might be and what results they had in response to treatment. Sometimes this only tells what it is not but all information is useful.

Listening and Smelling

In human practice, the first of these means listening to the sound of someone's voice – not just what they say but how they say it. Is it as if they are shouting at you? Are they laughing or crying? This is really not applicable for horses. Certainly all horses have a different 'voice' but interpreting it is another matter. However, we can listen to the horse's footsteps and see if one leg lands heavier than the others.

We know nowadays that dogs can detect illness in people by smell but this was also a technique used as a cornerstone of oriental diagnosis. Again, this cannot be used so easily in horses but occasionally you can walk into a stable that looks spotlessly clean and think, this does not smell good.

Observation

Since we are not able to fully utilise the first two of these cornerstones, observation is a very important tool in working out what is happening. Simply put, anything that deviates from our perfectly balanced horse is of interest. Sometimes things are very noticeable but on other occasions, something can appear quite minor yet that small point may lead to a big change. First we can look at the topics mentioned previously such as Yin or Yang and which Element the horse is both physically and mentally. Of almost equal importance are areas of tension, areas of over- or under-developed muscle, and how the horse stands.

Stances

Different imbalances within each different channel will result in a different stance or in some cases as a mix of two. This is not as strange as it may sound. If you have an elderly horse with arthritic changes then there will be an imbalance in the channel associated with the joints but you might also have the knock-on effect, or perhaps primary effect, of an imbalance in the channel associated with ligaments and tendons. It is therefore not unusual for the horse to have one hind leg in one direction and the other one showing something else.

A twenty-eight-year-old horse showing excellent abdominal muscles for his age, but some tension in the hindquarters.

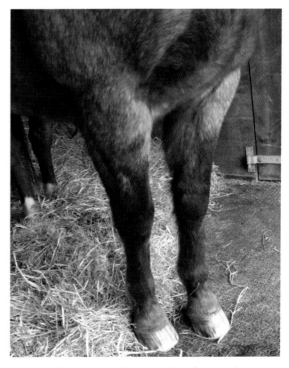

A stance showing very close-together front and hind legs.

A stance showing legs that are too wide apart.

Tension

Areas of tension are often found around point of hip, the top of the neck and at the withers. Often these three can appear together because if the horse is unable or unwilling to use his hindquarters correctly then he will not use his core muscles, which can result in either the horse pulling himself along by the front end or hollowing through the back, not lifting the shoulders and raising the head and neck instead.

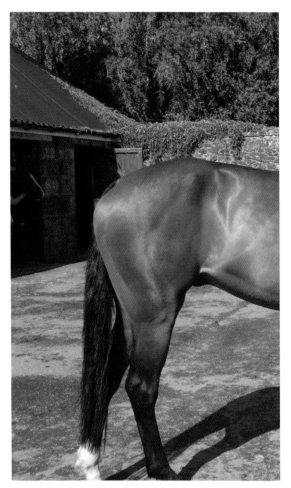

Tension around the tuber coxae.

Manes and Tails

The mane should fall to one side but often there are splits in the mane. The two most commonly found are a small part at the top of the neck over the atlas/axis and this is often accompanied by another small part near the withers. Many people wrongly attribute this to rugs but it indicates misalignments as the neck goes one way and then tries to counteract this by going the other way in an effort to remain straight. The other split is usually found in the middle of the neck in line with a single misalignment or tension.

The tail should be relaxed and straight. It is after all an extension of the spine. If the tail is clamped, it may indicate an issue in the sacrum or the spine.

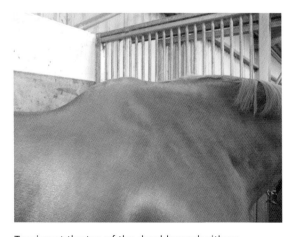

Tension at the top of the shoulder and withers.

If the horse holds his tail to one side then he is protecting that side. You sometimes find that when on a circle the horse will hold his tail to the inside and when the direction is changed so is the tail, so that it once again is on the inside. This means that when the weight is on the inside leg, it causes discomfort and so either there is a problem in both hind legs or it is something going on in the pelvic area.

Coat

There are many interesting things that can be deduced from looking at the coat but unfortunately many of them may have other meanings. Changes of colour and changes of direction in the coat can be interesting, as well as where the horse may itch or chew. Often these are along the channels and the horse is doing his own Shiatsu. However, one of the most clear-cut pieces of information that we can get from the coat is by looking at the dirty bits. Of course, after rolling it is common to see mud or grass around point of hip, at the top of the scapula and at the top of the neck, but does it only appear on one side? It is easy to dismiss this as just coincidence because these are the areas that are prominent but horses can have mud patches in some strange areas and they are quite deliberate.

The coat is disturbed where the horse has nibbled to release something along the Spleen channel.

Lovely mud marks where the horse has rubbed to release something, as well as an interesting mane.

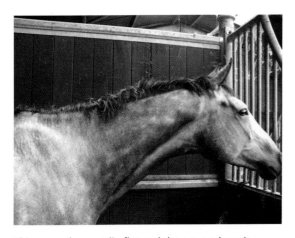

This mane does not lie flat and the areas where it changes direction correspond to weakness in the neck.

Hooves

When it come to the hoof, there are so many things to look at including quality of hoof, angles of the hoof and shod or barefoot to mention a few. From an Equine Shiatsu perspective, however, we look at cracks and indents. In terms of practice, we stop at the coronet band because of the difficulty in feeling anything through the hoof wall but that rather assumes that the hoof is dead, which patently it is not. Therefore the channels will run down all the way to the ground and if you have a channel that

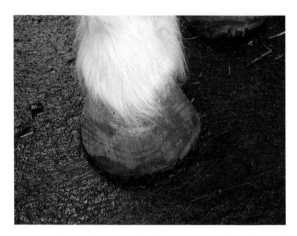

Dips, cracks and flares in the hoof are a continuation of imbalance in the channel above.

is out of balance then often there will be a crack or indentation running onwards from the coronet band downwards.

Facial Diagnosis

Facial diagnosis – looking at colours and lines on the face – was mentioned in Chapter 2 but here we can talk more about how this can be used in horses. It is possible to find some interesting lines on the face of a horse but this relates more to craniosacral therapy. Comparing a human diagnostic feature with an equine one leads us to bags under the eyes. We noted earlier that bags under the eyes are an imbalance in the Kidney channel. This channel has many different functions, but two of the most widely found relate to the joints and also the endocrine system. If you see this in a very young horse or a very old horse, then it might be reasonable to conclude that one is still growing and the other has wear and tear in the joints. However, if you find these bags in a younger horse, then the next question should be, has there ever been any sign of laminitis? Bags under the eyes are often found in EMS and PPID horses and indeed when a crisis is nearing the bags get bigger before any other symptoms.

Common symptoms, such as runny noses and mucky eyes and ears, also have correspondences with different channels; all these things added together help to build a bigger picture of where the source of the imbalances might be.

Many of the facial diagnosis symptoms described above can be observed while the horse is not moving but there are other things that can be picked up through movement.

Observation through Movement

For many people, observation of movement tends to be limited to the legs but there is so much more we can look at. We have already mentioned footfall and tails when the horse is moving, but we can also see how easily he can turn his neck in both directions. Is the head staying perpendicular or does it tilt? We can also look at the swing in the ribs and the movement of the pelvis.

If you can watch a horse rolling, there are a few questions worth considering:

- Does he get down and up on the same side?
- Does he roll on both sides, or only one?
- Can he get all the way over?

People sometimes think that a horse is reluctant to roll if they have a bad back but, in my opinion, it has more to do with the confidence that his legs will get him back up again.

The next thing to observe is how they stand when urinating, especially geldings. Can they stand evenly with both hind feet the same, or do they rest or twist one of them? They should be able to stretch out evenly. Another important and very telling observation is that of the jaw while the horse is eating. Does it swing easily and evenly from side to side? Everything means something and even if it is not obvious what that meaning is, it might be worth investigating. While there may not be a serious problem at the time, it means that something is not right and this may then lead to something that becomes a serious problem later on.

The channels have many functions but they also affect the area of the body through which they flow. This means that although every horse is an individual, there are also patterns that are commonly found in terms of biomechanics, and this can be looked at from an anatomical viewpoint.

Biomechanics of Movement

Bones, muscles, tendons and ligaments work together to determine how the horse moves; which one or ones of these are the original source of any problem will vary. Here we can look at some common problems and possible causes.

The Skeleton

The two crucial factors here are symmetry and straightness. It is also important to consider the difference between posture and confirmation. Confirmation is the actual shape of the skeleton, which means the length and density of the bone, the shape of the eyes, the length of the ears and those things that cannot be changed. Things like being straight in the hind legs, elbows in so that the front feet point outwards, roach back are all postural issues and these can be restored to a correct posture.

The Magic of Equine Shiatsu

When trying to find a horse to photograph to show facial misalignment, I took my camera to see a horse with just that at his first session. When I got there, however, the facial misalignment was gone! Interestingly, because the horse had other, more pressing issues to deal with, I had not worked much on his face, except to try to release some jaw tension.

It is also a common misconception that to realign structural imbalance you need an osteopath or a chiropractor. While Shiatsu works well with both of these therapies, it can also stand alone to help skeletal issues.

The Face

Asymmetry is more common in the face than most people imagine and the causes are multiple. If you stand directly in front of your horse and compare the two sides of his face, they should be almost mirror images of each other. Total perfection is not natural but it should not be obviously different between one side and the other. The easiest things to look at first are the eyes and the nostrils. Are they the same size? Are they equidistant from the midline? Are they level? The cheekbones, temporomandibular joint (TMJ) and occiput are also easy areas to check for asymmetry.

Some of the landmarks that can be checked for symmetry in the face.

The reasons why a horse may not be symmetric are numerous. Birth trauma as the head is pushed out and trauma due to injury account for many of these, but they can also be the result of a problem elsewhere. TMJ issues are a major source of facial asymmetry and this can occur from dental problems, incorrect biting, poll tension, asymmetry elsewhere in the body and even bad riding. If your horse does not like being touched on the face or does not yawn properly, or even at all, then take a close look at his face.

The Neck

There may be only seven cervical vertebrae but they can cause lots of trouble. It is important to remember that the last few vertebrae are actually hidden within the thoracic sling and are therefore impossible to influence directly. It also means that they are often forgotten about. Misalignments can be found at any point, or even several points, down the neck. The neck has four distinct movements – up, down, in and out. Horses with tension in the head often hold their necks in the up position, or up and in, and are incapable of the out movement. Horses with back or pelvic pain will not be able to move down properly and as compensation may also get stuck in the up and in position.

We also want the horse to be able to bend correctly and that does not mean carrot stretches but rather a gentle bend to left and right while keeping the head perpendicular. It is not that carrot stretches are not useful but they can disguise an inability to give a nice bend while riding.

In Traditional Oriental Medicine the neck is seen as the bridge between the brain and the legs. If you consider horses that weave or crib, there are distinctive neck and leg actions.

The Shoulders

Unevenness in the shoulders, where both scapulae are not at the same height or angle, can lead to a great many problems. Because a horse does not have a collarbone, the whole thoracic sling should be able to move up and down with ease, but when the horse is not correctly aligned in his shoulders this is not possible. The strides will not be even, the back cannot extend and stretch and often this then leads to the kind of misalignments already mentioned.

The Spine

When we look at the thoracic vertebrae, we must also consider the ribs as they should swing evenly from side to side. The whole back should be able to rock gently and independently from side to side. The major movement of the spine is to move up and down and problems in this area, which include kissing spines, are solely the remit of the veterinary profession. That said, enabling the spine to move from side to side can be helped with Equine Shiatsu. However, it is true that mostly this is the result of another problem somewhere else in the body, either from external circumstances such as a badly fitting saddle or an internal problem such as ulcers or leg problems. The latter is something that often results in problems within the lumbar spine. The thoracic spine is protected in part by the ribs, and the sacrum and pelvis have huge muscle mass around them to help stabilise them. The lumbar spine is the weak link and if you have a horse that is even slightly uneven in stride length then this makes the horse crooked and something has to give. An interesting exercise is to stand your horse up square and then look down on his spine from behind and above. Any curvature or twist should be considered something of note.

The Pelvis

Unevenness in the pelvis can be seen as a tilt or a rotation. In either case the result is a horse that cannot use the hindquarters as the powerhouse that creates dynamic forward movement. The most common signs that something is wrong are a dip in front of the tuber sacrale in the midline and different heights on either side of the tuber sacrale. These are easily seen but you can also draw a line from the highest point on the tuber coxae to the spine from both sides; both lines should meet at exactly the same spot.

The Tail

In Equine Shiatsu the tail is considered to be a mirror of the neck. The top of the tail corresponds to the bottom of the neck and the end of the tail relates to the top of the neck. Misalignments can be found and worked here in horses whose necks are too sore to touch. It is also worth remembering that the tail is part of the spine and in a healthy spine with no problems, the tail will be straight, relaxed and easy to lift. In contrast, tails that are clamped and crooked can be an extension of what is happening in the spine. In the practical part of this book, there are many techniques that can address these issues.

The Musculature

Muscle groups generally work in pairs, one to flex and one to extend. If one of these cannot work properly, either because it is too weak or because it has solidified, then the other will compensate by working harder than it should and become overdeveloped. As this topic is certainly another book in itself, we will look at a few general areas.

Common Problems

In a very simplistic explanation we can look at muscle groups in pairs:

• Back and front of the hind legs/hindquarters
• Top and bottom of the trunk
• Back and front and top and bottom of the front legs/shoulders
• Top and bottom of the neck

The Hindquarters

When we see musculature that is out of balance in one area of the body, there will be a knock-on effect throughout the rest of the body, to a greater or lesser degree depending on what is actually going on or what has happened in the past. Starting with the hindquarters, we are simply looking for a good, round shape. This is the powerhouse, or the engine, and if your engine is faulty, there will be many other problems. Several groups of muscles are involved in this process. There are three gluteal muscles – the superficial, the medial and the deep – which act to extend the hip to create propulsion. Also involved in hip and stifle extension, needed to power the engine of the horse, are the biceps femoris, semi-tendinosis and semi-membranosis, more commonly referred to as the hamstrings. These are all part of the dorsal chain of muscles, all of which help to allow the horse to stretch and extend.

The Hind Legs

However, you can find horses with well-rounded hindquarters who lack power because of hind leg issues. In these cases, you often find tight, overdeveloped hamstrings, as the legs are going up and down like pistons, but not forward. Because the forward movement is not correct, the horse then lacks muscle at the front of the leg, which is involved in lifting the leg to enable it to come forward. The tensor fascia latae (TFL), which runs from the tuber coxae to the stifle, the quadriceps group, of which the TFL is part, and the iliopsoas group, which attaches to the lumbar spine, are all involved in flexing the hip, creating movement within the pelvis to allow the hind leg to come under the body. If the muscles that lift the leg are not functioning correctly then the horse may develop tension in the lumbar area as the iliopsoas muscles become overworked. However, when the abdominals lift the trunk, the back needs to be able to stretch and allow this. Any problems within the spine or the muscles supporting the spine, the longest of which is the longissimus dorsi, will make this more difficult.

The Back and the Abdominals

If your horse has a tight back, he cannot extend and if he has ineffective abdominal muscles, he will not be able to lift his core. These two usually go hand in hand, but the question is which one is the cause and which the effect. In the photograph ABOVE, there is an elderly horse with a roach back and this limits his ability to use his abdominals correctly. Given that he has been like this for a long time, the scope for improvement is limited but we can make him more comfortable and prevent more tension from accumulating. However, you can also see the knock-on effect on his shoulders and, in particular, the thoracic trapezius muscle.

The Shoulders

The muscles primarily involved in lifting the shoulders are the trapezius muscles, cervical and thoracic, but the muscles of the thoracic sling are also involved. In order for a horse to carry itself

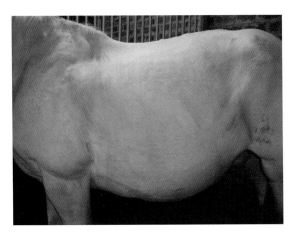

Having a roach back, this horse finds it difficult to lift the abdominals because his back cannot stretch as it should.

correctly, these muscles, which include the four pectoral muscles and the serratus ventralis thoracis, need to be able to contract and lift the whole shoulder. Behind the scapula is the latissimus dorsi, which supports the back and helps bring the trunk over the front leg when it moves forward. The splenius muscle, which is part of the ventral chain, extends to allow this lift, which in turn allows the neck to extend and lift.

If the horse lacks muscle through the trapezius then he is not using these muscles to help lift the thoracic sling. Usually, this results in tight and often overdeveloped pectoral muscles, resulting in horses that do not like being touched on the chest or that lack the ability to abduct the front leg. A common cause of problems in the trapezius muscles is an ill-fitting saddle. If this is the reason then it may be that the rest of the muscles from the hindquarters forward are fine, but without the ability of the shoulders to lift and open, they cannot work correctly even if physically they can.

The Front Legs

When a horse is not able to power through from behind, the default position is to pull themselves along with the front legs. There are two things that are seen most commonly. The first is an over-developed brachiocephalicus, giving the classic upside-down look to the horse. This can also occur when the horse has something to pull against such as a martingale. Even if you now ride with a very loose martingale, the mere feeling of wearing it will make the horse think that he has something to brace against, if he has done so in the past, thus continuing a vicious circle. Because the abdominals have not lifted and the back stretched out, in order for the trunk to move forward, the horse will overuse his latissimus dorsi muscles. In some horses, usually native types, this area can be quite well developed naturally but if you see a big bulge behind the scapula on a thoroughbred type of horse then this should be a big red flag.

The Neck

The neck being the last part of this cycle of movement has many places where it can go wrong for a variety of reasons. The brachiocephalicus, mentioned above, also raises the head and neck, as well as moving the head from side to side. However, there are many layers of muscle in the neck, making it a complicated part of the body. Neck tensions can come from behind and move forward, as already mentioned, but they can also come from the head and move backwards. Problems in the TMJ or the hyoid apparatus can affect tiny muscles that go up towards the poll and also the sternohyoid and sternocephalicus muscles, which in turn affect the shoulder. The neck should be a smooth extension of the back and so upside-down necks, tension along the top of the neck, over high head carriages and dips in front of the wither are all indications of something out of balance.

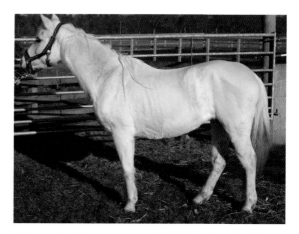

A horse showing a pattern of imbalance from back to front.

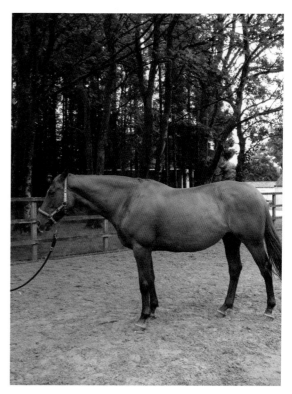

A horse showing the resulting musculature from having a foal.

A horse with very poor musculature.

The first photograph (left) shows almost all of the incorrect musculature previously mentioned, whereas the second photograph has more specific areas to consider. Beginning at the hindquarters, there is a noticeable dip on the topline at the insertion point for the biceps femoris, and the hindquarters themselves could be rounder. The hamstrings are defined enough to be seen and there is also tension in the front of the hind leg. The abdominals do not show an obvious problem, but the shoulder looks bottom-heavy, with a lack of muscle at the withers and overdevelopment of the pectorals. This, combined with the front legs being noticeably back under the horse, shows overdevelopment in the brachiocephalicus and tension along the top of the neck.

The third photograph shows the fewest problems but there is always something to look at. Rather than initially looking at specific areas of musculature, try to imagine how you would like this horse to change to create a perfect picture. This horse needs to raise the shoulder and this in turn will help to lift the abdominals, which will then encourage her to use her hindquarters more effectively. She gave birth about a year before this photograph was taken and that explains the reason why her abdominals are not as they should be. With correct work, and some help from Shiatsu, she should quickly rebuild her core strength. This is, as stated at the start of the Common Problems section, a rather simplistic view of what is happening, but keeping things simple helps to train your eye as to the areas that are not working as they should.

Musculature that is working too hard is often sensitive, or even painful. When there is a skeletal misalignment, the horse will not be able to move correctly and smoothly. When asked to move correctly, the horse will evade, resist or fight back. Knowing how to interpret warning signs before they become actions, and having the ability to react accordingly, is essential to a good relationship and interaction with the horse.

Reading the Horse

Horses generally give many little subtle signals when they are worried or concerned about what you are doing or are about to do. Picking up on these signs and instantly reacting to them is the way in which the horse will realise that we are listening and can be trusted. When you have established this trust, they are more likely to let you into the areas about which they are most anxious. Sometimes this anxiety is because of pain but sometimes it is memory of pain, which is more difficult to deal with, as the original pain no longer exists.

Signs of Anxiety

- Sudden tension or flinching
- Raising the head high often with much jaw tension
- Eating more quickly
- Moving away
- Hiding a part of their body from you
- Holding their breath
- A worried look in the eyes
- Threatening to kick or bite

While appearing to show interest, there is an anxious look in the eyes.

61

Signs of Warning

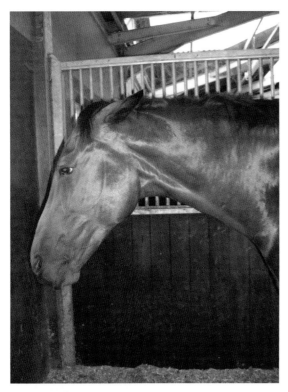

The classic ears-back warning.

- Trying to kick or bite
- Ears back
- Squashing or pushing
- Tail swishing
- Foot stamping

If you notice any of these then reduce the pressure and slow down or stop immediately; only continue when the horse has relaxed and offered to let you start again. However, when you begin again, go slower and more gently and only build up as and when the horse is happy. If he does not accept what you are trying to do then try another way. Perhaps go back to the step before or use a different technique, but proceed with caution and great care. When the horse lets go and is happy with your touch, then hopefully you will see signs of contentment.

Signs of Contentment

A lovely and relaxed horse with a soft eye.

- Eyes closing
- Deep breathing
- Sighing
- Head dropping
- Yawning
- Whole body relaxation
- Stretching of their own volition
- Mutual grooming

For some horses, the ability to let go and relax in front of people is very difficult as they may see it as a sign of weakness, especially if they have been carrying a lot of tension for many years. In this situation, they wait until you have gone and can often be found lying down sleeping shortly afterwards.

The ability and awareness to react to what the horse is telling you is a major part of good quality of touch but there are other important points to consider as well.

Quality of Touch

If you have good quality of touch, then it is easier to feel what is happening as well as enhancing the interaction with the horse. To help tune in to achieve this, you will need to be aware of the techniques covered in this section. There are many people who work with Ki who will tell you that they do not feel anything – they just know that the horse does. Despite the fact that they believe that they feel nothing, however, they undoubtedly use the following techniques. We touched on why these were important in Chapter 2 but here we can look at the more practical application.

Posture and Breathing

Being able to breathe and correct spinal alignment go hand in hand. Breathing is a powerful tool in Shiatsu and must never be underestimated. A useful exercise is to sit squarely on a chair, making sure that both seat bones are evenly set, and gently allow your spine to stretch up vertebra by vertebra, from the bottom up, as if you were building blocks one on top of the other. When you get to the top of the neck, imagine that something is lifting the crown of your head to place the skull on the spine; because the spine is curved, this will leave you looking slightly downwards and not straight ahead.

Next take a deep breath and feel it move all the way down into your abdomen. With each intake of breath, allow the feeling of warmth and strength to build within the Hara. Be comfortable with this and

What Does Ki Feel Like?

What each individual feels is a completely personal thing and will vary from person to person. Therefore, what I can talk about is what I feel and this may not be what you feel. Sometimes you can feel a hot or cold draught as a result of Ki but it can be difficult to know if what you are feeling is not just a breeze, given that horses generally do not live in airtight places. In some cases, you can feel as if you are being pulled into the body, and in other cases, as if you are being pushed away. For me, balanced Ki feels like a gentle buzzing or tingling going on under your fingers or palm. When Ki is in excess, it can be more like a frantic wasps' nest. In contrast, when it is deficient, in the beginning there may be nothing, but with patience and some breathing, things gradually come to life. When things feel the same in both hands, that area is balanced.

On occasion, especially if things have been very deficient for a long time, you may not feel that enough is happening, but it is a start and that is progress. When this happens, sometimes in the next session it may feel very busy and in excess; this can be because things have swung in the opposite direction, like when you have freezing cold hands, you warm them, and suddenly you have pins and needles as your circulation returns.

Do not try to feel Ki; just let it happen. The first time that I felt something, I was immediately thinking about what I felt and therefore not in Hara, not breathing, and the feeling disappeared. The harder you try, the more elusive it can become but also remember that even if you do not feel anything, you can still work with Ki by reading the horse, who certainly feels it.

do not force the breathing. This is an exercise that can be done to calm the mind or to prepare for a Shiatsu session, but also as you become more comfortable with it you can learn to breathe out into your hands to move and project Ki. This takes time to perfect and needs concentration on the breathing because if you become distracted then your breathing will become shallow and ineffective.

Keeping the Horse's Attention with Two-Handed Connection

In Zen Shiatsu, both hands work together and horses tend to find this reassuring as they are then aware of where your hands are and what they are doing. The working hand is the one that moves along the channels and all too easily the supporting hand can become slightly ignored. However, it is important to keep the supporting hand focused, especially in a horse that lacks attention and is easily distracted or is trying to avoid or distract you. When you feel the same 'life' in both hands then the Ki is balanced and you can move on. Be aware that sometimes this can take time and is not something that will happen immediately.

Why the Correct Angle of Pressure is Important

When working the channels, pressure needs to be at 90 degrees in order to connect directly with the Ki. Pressure that is not at the right angle will not respond to the pressure and indeed, a sensitive being like a horse will know that it does not feel as it should and will often move away. Sometimes this is because they do not like what they feel but sometimes they are trying to get you into the right position.

Consideration must be made for the shape of the horse and the angle at which he stands on each leg. In order for you to be in the correct position, you need to think not only about your hands but the whole of

Fingers at a 90-degree angle of pressure over the back.

Fingers at 90 degrees on a sloping wither.

your body. This will then help you to breathe correctly and move from Hara.

Moving from Hara to Find the Right Amount of Pressure

One of the benefits of moving from Hara is that it reduces the need for physical effort and this is most important when working with an animal as large as a horse. Tension anywhere within the body will cause restrictions and impact on the ability to connect with Ki. Keeping a wide stance to balance yourself, making sure that you can move each joint within your body, are relaxed and feel as if you can notice space within the joints, will help you to lean into the horse and determine the correct amount of pressure.

By using your whole body to move into the horse, you learn to feel at which point you need to stop. Sometimes the horse will lean into you, thereby dictating how much pressure is needed, and that makes things much easier. In this situation, a strong wall behind you is useful! Finding the correct level of pressure is very important, as not enough pressure will be ineffective at reaching Ki, and too much can be painful for the horse, which may cause him to tighten up to protect his body rather than unwind and let go.

Equine Shiatsu can benefit any horse but there are some contraindications for the level covered in this book, so please read the next section carefully before working on a horse.

Contraindications to Shiatsu Treatment

There are two types of indicators that need to be covered for when an Equine Shiatsu session is not appropriate. First, there are situations where a horse should not be worked at all:

- Infectious or contagious skin problems
- High fever
- Extreme fatigue
- When taking antibiotics and for ten days after
- When taking anti-inflammatories for an acute condition

Second, there are circumstances that are only suitable for experienced practitioners:

- Pregnant mares
- Very young horses – usually this means under five but please remember that a very large breed of horse can still be a baby at five

Playing with Custard

To help understand how much pressure is needed, we need to imagine a custard with a thick skin on it. We then want to be able to make the custard move. If we do not have enough pressure then our fingers will sit on the top and not move anything underneath; if we have too much pressure, our fingers will go through the skin of the custard, which is not an agreeable situation for anyone! A less graphic version of this is to say that we need to wait until we feel the body tell us that that is enough. We come to, and meet, the point of resistance but do not go beyond it.

- Horses under veterinary care for a specific condition or injury
- Care should also be taken with the very old as it is possible to do too much

Taking Care of the Giver

While there are no contraindications as such for the giver of Shiatsu, there some things of which you need to be aware.

Physical Problems

We all have strengths and weaknesses within our body that can help or hinder our Shiatsu. Being aware of what these are and making every effort to address these will obviously benefit the horse, as your session will be more relaxed and flowing. It is therefore your responsibility to look after yourself. You could get Shiatsu for yourself, or learn Tai Chi or Qi Gong, which will help your own well-being. The better we are within ourselves, the better it is for the horse too.

Emotional Issues

There are two things to consider when looking at your emotional state when giving Equine Shiatsu. First, there is the stress we bring from whatever is going on in our lives at the time. If you are feeling angry or distressed about something then you are not in the correct frame of mind to give good Shiatsu. However, this does not mean that you should not. The important point is that you must leave all that stress at the stable door. If you can do this and spend time where it is just you and the horse, with no outside worries or distractions, then a Shiatsu session will be as beneficial to you as to the horse.

Second, when you are not sufficiently grounded or in Hara, it is easier to pick up sensations from the horse if there is a transfer of Ki between you.

Sometimes this can be a physical reaction such as a headache or feeling heat coming up your arms. If you notice this, simply break the connection and go and touch something natural such as stone or wood. Some people like to carry out a small ritual of washing their hands after a session, as if to cleanse completely. Besides a physical reaction, other people can pick up on emotional issues and, for example, find themselves in tears with no notion of why this should be. There are some people who are more sensitive to this sort of experience but the key to it all is to stay grounded, in Hara, and breathe. These things are relatively rare but if it happens to you, do not worry – just be aware that you might need to find a way to protect yourself, and sometimes that is as simple as wearing a hat!

So let's get started…

My Story

When I was about eight or nine, I somersaulted over my father's horse's neck, landed on my feet and then sat down on my ankle. I was cantering down a steep hill with no saddle or bridle, just a halter, and I have to say in my defence, I was doing fine until he changed direction! In any case, my ankle was X-rayed but due to my young age, they could not tell if it was broken or not. It was strapped up and I was told to keep walking on it. About forty-five years later, it came back to haunt me.

I found that my ankle would swell badly and my extensor tendon would feel red hot. I tried various things to help but over time, it also led to a sore hip that would keep me awake at night. Things came to a head when, one night, I developed extremely painful sciatica and, having read stories of the number of painkillers that friends had been prescribed for that, I decided I had to do something. The short version is that I sorted myself out in a day and now that I have addressed and continue to address any hip pain, my ankle is much better. It is still a bit more swollen than the other at the end of the day, but most of the pain has gone. I continue to address any issues that appear and I suspect that it is too late to eradicate the whole problem, but it is manageable, and it is also an example of how the effect can become part of the cause over time.

CHAPTER **6**

The First Steps

A Guide to a Practical Session

It is important to note that the techniques in Chapters 6–10 are not set out as a rigid protocol to be followed in a specific order. While each technique is designed to make the next one easier, it is possible that some horses dislike certain techniques or have no need of them. The order in which the areas of the body are worked will also vary from horse to horse. I would strongly suggest that the practical work in this chapter, which focuses on the body sweep and the Bladder channel, is the best place to start. After that, however, it can vary as to whether you begin with the hindquarters, the shoulders, the middle or even the head. Allow yourself to trust your intuition and be guided by it. If you make a mistake, the horse will tell you and you can change to another area.

You may decide that it is best to deal with the area where the horse has the most discomfort first to make him feel better and more relaxed. Similarly you might want to leave this until the end when you have managed to hopefully establish the trust of the horse, although you may find that you run out of time and the horse decides that he has had enough before you have successfully addressed the issue. There is no right or wrong in this matter and it just depends on the horse. However, I would say that if your horse is *very* distressed or angry about being touched in a certain place, then that is not the best, or safest, place to begin.

We need also to consider how often a horse will need a Shiatsu session. The advantage of working on your own horse is that you can also do mini sessions just to check, and address, any issues that you are aware of before riding.

Hockney

Hockney was a retired event horse that I had on loan some years ago. As an ex-competition horse he had various little problems that became more noticeable with age. One of these led to him being tight in one shoulder and so, before any lesson, I would check out his shoulder for tension and, if necessary, do some techniques to loosen and relax the area. This meant that we could start the lesson able to work correctly and so benefit from the whole time, rather than spending the first half of the lesson getting him to relax and soften before being able to work correctly.

How Often Should My Horse Receive Shiatsu?

Unfortunately, there is no absolute answer to this question. It depends on his level of work, what his problems are and how deep-seated those problems have become. However, there are two things that are true when it comes to the question of how regularly a horse receives Shiatsu. First, it is possible to give them too much. This then becomes system-overload and the horse will not receive the benefit that he should. The second truth is that the more you give them Shiatsu, the less regularly they will need it unless their work level changes or their issues become more problematic, such as with age.

With the techniques in this book, you can start with an interval of a week to ten days between sessions and then lengthen this out to three weeks to monthly. I generally see my clients on a six-weekly rotation but with some clients it can be as long as two to three months between sessions. However, the kind of session given by a practitioner will be much more profound and therefore longer lasting. For someone working on their own horse, it is simpler to say that often the horse will tell you when they need your assistance as they become more bodily aware and know that you can help. And so, to start…

The Practicalities

How and Where to Practise

Each choice of where and when to give Equine Shiatsu has its drawbacks and so compromise to find what works best for you and your horse is required. For some, the easiest place will be in the stable but sometimes this can restrict the amount of space required. Also, yards can be busy with many distractions and in some cases horses will use these as a chance to try to not think about what is happening to them. Outside, in an arena or field, can equally provide distractions and may allow too much space.

Can I Tie the Horse Up?

Ideally the answer to this is no as it is better for the horse to know that he has freedom of choice and can move away. Indeed, many people like to work without a halter or any kind of restraint. However, I personally like the horse to wear a halter but not have the horse tied. That way I can have some control if the horse becomes unhappy or worried but they can still move away if they want to. Very occasionally, it is necessary to tie them but this needs to be done with a long rope so they can still move away, turn and look at you, and stretch their necks as you work.

And so to start…

The Body Sweep

You are probably quite used to feeling down your horse's legs for heat, swelling, lumps or bumps. Well, why stop at the legs? When we give a full body sweep, it can tell us many things and likewise can tell the horse about us. The amount of pressure given is important as it is the first connection with the horse; if it is too light and too fast then the horse will be able to ignore you if, for some reason, he does not feel inclined to become involved. If it is too slow or too intense then it may be painful in some areas and that is not the best way to get started.

Places where the horse tries to avoid your touch or is unhappy with it initially tell us two things. First, that there is a problem that needs to be addressed in that area, and second, that we need to be aware of our own safety when addressing it. So, what are we looking for?

- Areas of hot or cold
- Musculature that is too hard or too soft
- Changes of direction, texture or appearance of the coat
- Anywhere that the horse tries to avoid being touched

In the last of this list, the most common reactions are for horses to raise their heads to avoid the head or top of the neck and a dislike to being touched on the flanks or inner hind leg, when the hind leg may threaten. Some horses are also very sensitive around their pectoral muscles, when the teeth may come into play, and so all of these show that while there is an issue to be dealt with, care and sensitivity is required for our own safety as well as the well-being of the horse. However, not all reactions are extreme and so it is important to observe your horse's face as much as possible throughout the body sweep. In some places, you might just get a quick flick of an ear or a wrinkle in the nostril to express displeasure or concern. Likewise, there may be areas that the horse really enjoys and the eyes grow heavy and close or there is a release of breath. Everything is of interest and worthy of note.

Relax. Breathe. Begin.

Start as close to the top of the neck that the horse is comfortable with and stroke down in long sweeping movements, one hand at a time, while never losing contact with the horse. Try not to cover an

area more than once and pay close attention to the horse's expression and your own breathing. Continue over the shoulder and down the front leg. When moving down the leg, it is better to end up in a squatting position rather than bent over as it is easier to breathe when you are not folded in half. Maintaining contact as you rise, come up to the withers and stroke along the back and abdomen, remembering to cover under the belly as well as the sides. Stroke down over the hindquarters and the hind legs, sweep the tail and come around to the other side. Walk your hands up the body to the top of the neck and begin the second side. Finish with a tail sweep.

Notice any differences between one side and the other and what your horse enjoys and what areas he may be more worried or even indifferent about. This technique is incredibly simple but it is also important as it is your initial contact with the horse and it is important to get it right. It will help both you and the horse relax, which means that you can then move smoothly on to the Bladder channel.

Beginning the body sweep at the head.

69

Continuing the body sweep over the rest of the body.

Body sweep over the hindquarters before going down the legs.

Location of Bl channel.

The Bladder Channel

The Bladder channel runs along the back, parallel to the dorsal spine, and as such is an area of immense importance on the horse. It is one of the longer channels and runs from one end of the horse to the other, and so its influence can affect the whole horse. It is also a channel that is directly affected by outside factors such as the saddle, the bridle and the rider. Working the Bladder channel has many benefits and the complete beginner can make some amazing changes without more specific theoretical knowledge. This is because from the withers back, there are important acupoints, known as Yu points, that are associated with the other primary channels in the body. By working on the Bladder channel, therefore, you are in effect working on all of the channels. It is not important at this stage to know exactly where these points are because if you are in Hara and relaxed in your own body, you will naturally fall into the places you need to be.

Although the Bladder channel begins just above the inside corner of the eye, it is preferable to start your Shiatsu at the withers. The reasons for this are that first, most horses are quite comfortable with being handled and touched in this area. Second, many horses have issues with their head and neck, and we do not really want to begin with a problem. Last, in Zen Shiatsu we like to work from the middle of the body out and so we can work from the withers to the hind hooves and then withers to head. From an energetic viewpoint, this is also the easier way to work. For example, if you have a horse with tension in the poll or an atlas/axis problem, if you start at the head, the horse will usually raise his head and neck to avoid your touch, which in turn causes a blockage energetically at the withers. Also, if you have something happening in these areas, it is usually an excess of Ki and the quickest way to get rid of it is by the shortest route, which is at the front.

Palming the Channel

In theory, you want to begin on the 'easy' side, where the horse is more comfortable and happier to accept your touch. This is true of all areas of the body but sometimes, when working along the back, it is not simple to tell which side the horse will prefer. In this case, start with the side being presented to you because horses have a tendency to hide their discomfort and make it more difficult for you to work. One of their most common tricks is to stand too close to the wall so that there is not enough room for a stretch!

If you place your hands on the horse's back so that the last joint of your fingers sits over the top of the dorsal spinous processes, you will find that the heel of your hands sits quite naturally into the line that is the Bladder channel. Obviously, if you have very small hands or a very small horse, then it may be easier to simply feel down from the top of the spinous processes towards the top of the ribs until you find a dip in the muscle.

Starting from the withers, please remember the golden rules:

• Two-handed connection
• 90-degree angle of pressure
• Moving from Hara

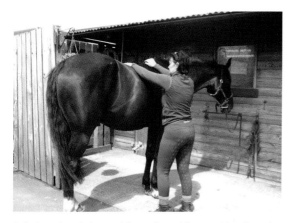

Palming the Bl channel from the withers, with relaxed shoulders and hands, using body movement.

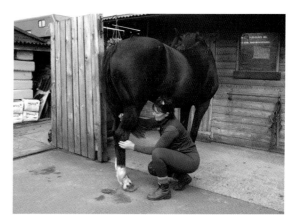

Moving on to the legs, the pressure comes from the fingers but here the supporting hand is not on the channel as it should be.

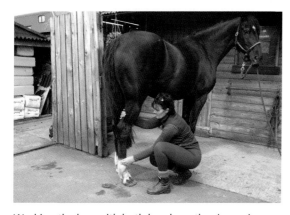

Working the legs with both hands on the channel.

Resting for a moment at the end of the channel.

How to Find Two-Handed Connection

The hand nearer the horse's head will stay in the same place until the hands become shoulder-width apart. This hand is still, listening and Yin. The other hand moves along the horse's back in approximately hand-width increments. When the hands become shoulder-width apart, slide the supporting hand up to the active, questioning Yang hand and continue. If you have a smaller horse, it is possible to continue like this until you reach the tail before turning to work down the hindquarters and legs. If you have a larger horse, you will need to turn when you reach the start of the hindquarters. In this case, or when you reach the tail as previously mentioned, turn your back to the horse's head so that your feet are now pointing rearwards and parallel to the horse. This last point is most important in order to achieve the correct angle of pressure. Even if one of your feet is pointing in a slightly different direction, it will alter the way you can move your hips and pelvis and thus change the angle of pressure. Horses are extremely sensitive and they will recognise that this is not quite right and may move away, walk forward or backward, or possibly change the angle of their own leg to get you into the correct position. However, there are not many horses that will be this accommodating.

The supporting, still hand sits on the Bladder channel and the active, working hand moves towards the horse's head, and so your movement, to create the pressure, is backwards. In order to move correctly, your outside leg must be a step forward from the one closer to the horse. When you get to the top of the leg, the fingers are used rather than the palms; the supporting hand wraps itself around the inside of the leg so that the fingers sit along the channel and the other hand can work down to the

With correct footwork, the body can move backwards, allowing the fingers to connect at the right angle.

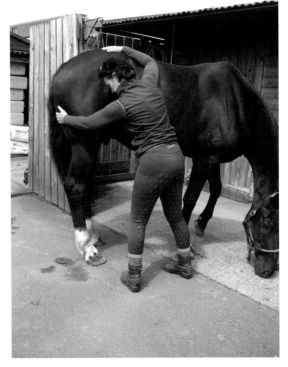

When the feet are not pointing in the correct direction, the body cannot move correctly.

coronet band. As you move down the leg, allow yourself to sink to the ground so that as you apply pressure you will find that you rock back on to your heels and come forward on to your toes as you move your working hand down each time. If the horse has long legs then, for comfort, you may need to move the supporting hand down to below the hock as you proceed. You also want to avoid the hands from becoming too far apart.

Finding the Correct Angle of Pressure for Different Shapes of Back

The angle of pressure needs to be 90 degrees and if your feet are correctly positioned as stated previously, this is relatively easy for working down the hind legs. However, working along the back is different. Some horses have flat tabletop backs, while others are quite sloping. The height of the horse will also make a difference in how you approach this. There is a tendency in beginners to want to push

down and, if the horse is very tall, they feel it necessary to try to reach up so they can push down. This is where moving from Hara comes into play (*see* the How to Move from Hara section BELOW). In any case, make sure that you are not pushing the horse over and causing him to sway as this means that your angle could be wrong and, probably, that you are pushing.

How to Move from Hara

This means that your pressure is coming from body movement and not through physical force through your fingers. The feeling for the receiver, in this case the horse, is quite different and the latter can feel intrusive and even painful. Allow your hands to be totally relaxed and just lean your weight into them. If your hands are up above your head on a tall horse then you may wonder how you can do that. This does take practice and even human Shiatsu practitioners who are used to working from Hara, but on someone

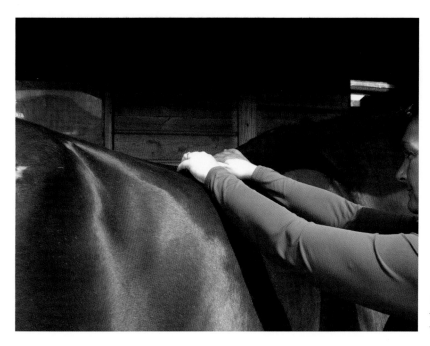

Finger pressure on Bl showing the correct 90-degree angle with good feet positioning.

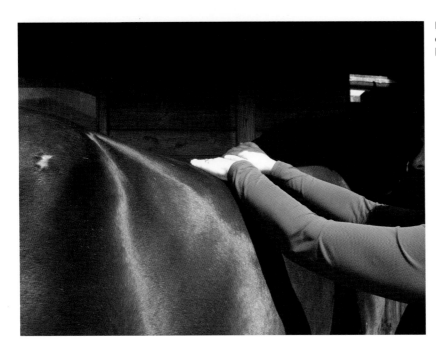

Incorrect angle of pressure on Bl channel means that the horse will be pushed over.

lying on the floor, can find this difficult. The answer is in the breathing.

First of all, we need to make sure that each joint in our body is relaxed and able to move. To begin with, it may be necessary to exaggerate the movement of your hips in order to ensure that they are really moving, especially if this feels strange to you. It is acceptable for your arms to rest and therefore touch the horse, as long as the focus of your pressure is through the heel of your hand at this stage and then through your fingers on the next passage. Take a big breath in as you move your working hand and release that breath as you connect again. This will allow you to sink into the horse's body until you feel it is far enough. This will vary depending on the quality of Ki under your hands at each moment. If the feeling is hard and unyielding, you will feel pushed away more quickly than if it is soft and lacking tonicity. In either case, trust your intuition as to whether to wait for longer or move on more quickly.

Where Ki is lacking, the sensation may be coolness, too much softness or just weakness and sometimes we need to wait in these places to 'wake them up' and get a feeling of life returning. If the area is hard or swollen then sometimes you need to wait to see if it will 'melt' under your hands, but on other occasions you need to move more quickly to get something to happen. Be guided by your horse as they will know what they need. It is not for you to decide what needs to be done but rather to work with your horse as it is his body and he knows how he feels more than you.

Finger Pressure on the Bladder Channel

Once the channel has been palmed, it can be repeated with finger pressure. This can be more intense and more precise, so you need to be more sensitive to the feedback you get from the horse, both in terms of facial expressions and body signals, and what you feel directly from the body under your fingers. Again, we begin by placing the supporting hand over the withers so that the palm sits into the channel. It is the working hand that uses the fingers by creating an arch so that the fingers are all in a line and they stay in the correct place. Line the fingers of the working hand up with the heel of the supporting hand to help you find where you should be. Remember to change your stance when you reach the hindquarters so that your angle of pressure stays correct.

Breathe out as you lean in and try not to spend all the time looking at your hands. Unfortunately, it is human nature to concentrate on our hands at this time but you can still feel what is happening without actually looking at your hands. Look instead at the horse's face. Not only will this give you feedback as to what he is feeling, it will let you know if he appreciates what is going on or not. If the answer is negative then change your way of working. Generally speaking, if the horse does not like what you are doing then it is probably too hard or too fast, or both. If your horse keeps moving away or is unhappy, just stop what you are doing and wait until he is ready for you to begin again but this time work more gently and more slowly. While he is moving, if possible, try to keep your supporting hand on the horse to maintain a connection. It is not always possible so if you break away completely, begin again very gently and quietly with one hand and then the other. If this new gentle approach is too soft, you can easily increase the pressure but pay close attention to the horse in order to work out when enough is enough.

Having completed the Bladder channel on the back, we could move to work from withers to head, but for now, it is probably easier just to do general neck work as shown in Chapter 10, which will address this part of the channel. The angles of pressure on the neck can be more difficult for someone who is new to this and there can also be tensions in the neck and poll that are better addressed further into the session. Therefore, having palmed and fingered the back and hind legs on one side, maintain contact with the horse and move round to repeat the process on the other side.

You should feel comfortable both during and after this work, and if any part of you is not then you are doing something wrong! The part of your body that is sore or aches is probably tense when you are working either because it is blocked and does not move freely or you are using muscular strength rather than body movement. And do not forget to breathe!

In the next chapter, we will look at working on the hindquarters but as already noted, you do not have to do this next. Feel free to choose another area to work if that is what you believe will be best for the horse.

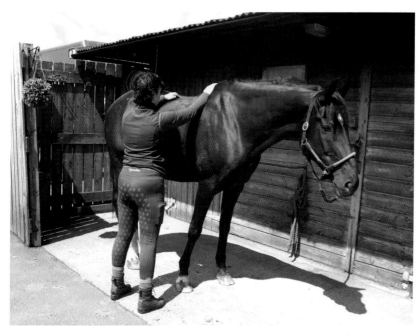

Finger pressure on the back.

Finger pressure with change of stance on hindquarters, with the horse beginning to relax.

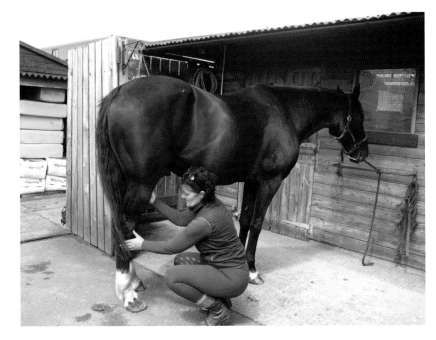

When using finger pressure on the legs, lower your body to bring the energy down.

CHAPTER 7

Loosening the Hindquarters

As each step is designed to make the next one easier for the horse, it would be best for you to follow the order set out here to begin with. As you become more familiar and competent with the techniques, you may find that, for example, your horse has beautifully loose and supple hamstrings, in which case you might decide that the technique for loosening them is not the best use of your time. Sometimes, however, you might find areas of tension or discomfort in the horse of which you were unaware. This may be because the horse has been hiding this issue, or has even forgotten about it as he adapts to a new way of moving, and now that you are having this conversation, it has been rediscovered.

Step 1: Moving Muscle

Before we attempt to perform more vigorous techniques, it is necessary to understand the quality of muscle over the hindquarters. This can be a one-handed or two-handed technique depending on what the horse is happy with. Start simply and begin with one hand working and, as always, one hand supporting. The supporting hand can rest on the Bladder channel over the lumbar area while the other hand gently moves the muscles over the top of the pelvis and sacrum. Gently lean the heel of the palm into the muscle until it fills your palm, rather like kneading bread or pastry. If your horse is happy with the

process, you can work deeper and, possibly, faster or with two hands at once. The musculature should feel pliable and elastic and move easily. If you find any tight knots, place your thumb over it at a 90-degree angle and sink down slowly, as and when the tension releases. Be patient and also be careful not to push, as this will be painful and the horse will tell you so! Remember to breathe.

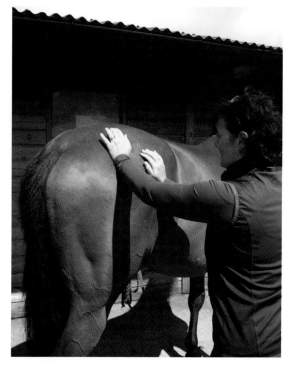

Moving muscle.

Step 2: Percussion

There are a variety of different ways of carrying out percussion techniques. Some use the hands separately and some as one unit, but whatever method you choose to try, the important point is that the shoulders and wrists need to be relaxed. This will result in the feeling that you are bouncing with the muscle rather than beating a drum.

Take care that you do not make too much noise as this can upset some horses. Whether it is actually the noise or an association with injections, it does not matter. If the horse is unhappy, lessen the distance between the top of your swing and the horse's body. Occasionally, the mere lifting of the hand, possibly after a memory of a beating, can result in the horse being upset. In this situation, place the relaxed fist on the horse and vibrate to cause a ripple within the muscle but without lifting your hand off the horse.

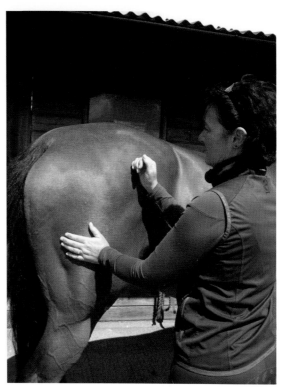

Percussion – keeping the hands on the body.

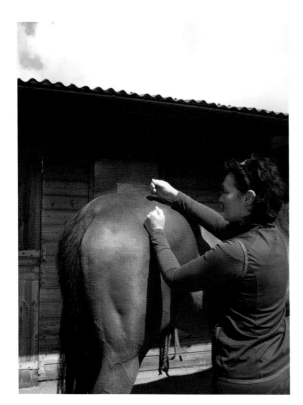

Percussion.

At the same time, do not be afraid to increase the speed and depth of the percussion if the horse is happy. In fact, the idea is to build up like a crescendo to just before the point where the horse says, that is enough. What you are looking for is the muscles to show movement all the way down the back and into the trapezius muscles. Initially, not many horses are actually capable of this.

If the back is very tight, then movement may stop where the back of the saddle would sit. More commonly is for it to stop where the rider sits, and only very few horses move all the way through the trapezius in the beginning. This is not a concern as such because hopefully any tension in these areas can be released with techniques used in the following chapters. However, if the horse finds it difficult to release or the situation does not improve with regular Shiatsu, it may be necessary to look for an external factor that prevents change for the better.

Step 3: Relaxing the Hamstrings (Semi-Tendinosis/ Semi-Membranosis)

This is a very important area to relax and can be extremely tight and tender to touch. If the horse has well-defined hamstrings, it basically means that his hind legs are going up and down like pistons but not really coming through. The horse will not be able to stretch his legs forward correctly because these muscles are tight; this means that his abdominals will not lift, the back will not stretch and the shoulders will end up pulling the torso forward and be unable to lift. The possible reasons for this are very numerous but observation of where the horse can and cannot move throughout the dorsal chain may give you some idea of what else is happening in the body and what techniques will help to release them.

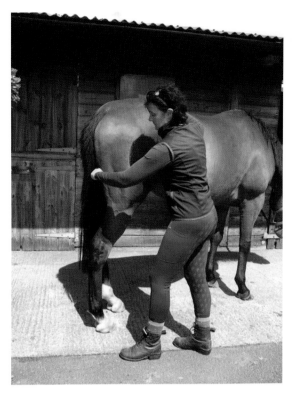

Relaxing the hamstrings from beside the horse.

Getting the Wobble

Trying to explain what Equine Shiatsu is, what it does and how it works in a very few words can be quite difficult and so I have been guilty of saying, somewhat flippantly, that Shiatsu is the art of getting the horse to wobble from one end to another. And, if he cannot, why not and what can you do about it? Perhaps this is a little demeaning to such a magical practice but at the same time, it sums it up quite well!

Gentle, Safe Muscle Movement

Because these muscles can be very tight and painful in some horses, test out how your horse reacts to touch with a safe method. Stand beside the hind leg, in the same position as you used to work down the Bladder channel, place one hand on the horse's back and lay a curled hand against the middle of the muscle. Gently vibrate so the muscle moves but do not take the hand away from the skin.

Being More Vigorous

If the horse is happy to accept this pressure and movement, and you feel safe to do so, without taking either hand off the horse, swivel round through 180 degrees so that you are now standing behind the horse, facing his head. This way you can keep watch on his head position and his ears as you continue to work. You can turn your working hand into a relaxed fist and continue to vibrate without lifting the hand off the horse, while staying in the middle of the muscle. You should be able to see movement down the horse's sides and into the shoulder.

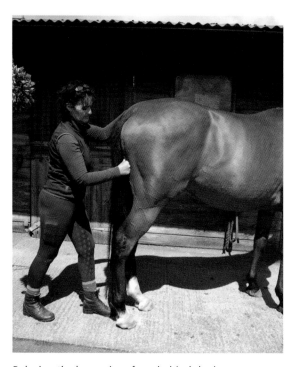

Relaxing the hamstrings from behind the horse.

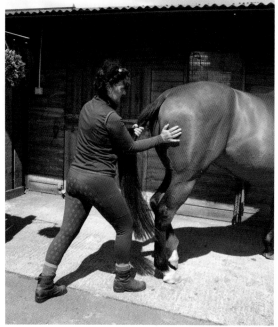

Palming down the hamstrings.

Palming the Hamstrings

First, take hold of the horse's tail in one hand. If you are going to work the hamstring on the left, hold the tail in the right hand. Take a step forward so that your left leg is forward; keep your back straight and upright. Your knees should be soft and able to bend as you descend down the muscles so that you end in a lunge position.

To begin, place the palm at the top of the hamstrings, beside the top of the tail, with the fingers pointing to the outside. Lean into the muscle with body weight and breathe out. Work your way down to the bottom of the muscles, taking great care as you get closer to the end as this is often the most sensitive part. You can repeat this two or three times if you feel it is necessary before moving on to thumbing down, which can be much more profound. Try to lower your body, keeping your back upright while descending rather than bending

over as this will impede your ability to breathe correctly.

Thumbing Down the Hamstrings

Having palmed down the back of the leg, the next stage is to thumb down. This time, turn your hand so the knuckles are on top but do not make a fist. Keep the fingers open and relaxed as you thumb down, again sinking your body downwards as you proceed. The important point here is to go in slowly but also to come out again at the same speed. This allows the horse time to decide if he wants to lean back into your pressure and therefore increase it. If this happens, try to wait until he moves off again as that is the horse's way of saying that he has had enough. However, having several hundred kilograms of horse sit on your thumb is not always pleasant, or even possible for some people, so there are other ways of dealing with this situation.

81

When They Try to Sit on You...

Horses that want a lot of pressure on their hamstrings have all sorts of tricks to keep you where they want you. The most common is to back you into the wall while they lean their whole weight on you. If you feel safe and your thumbs are strong enough, you can use the wall to brace against for as long as you can. However, if your thumbs cannot cope with this, turn your hand, make a fist and let them lean on your knuckles.

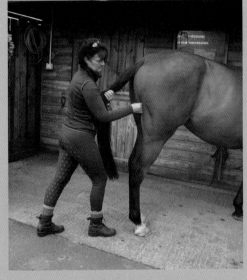

Using the fist on the hamstrings for horses that want to lean on you.

Often in this scenario, they will want you to do both sides at once and this is usually easier for you too.

It is important to come out just as slowly as you go in because if the horse is tentatively trying or considering increasing the pressure, you need him to be aware that you are moving away and give him time to think about it.

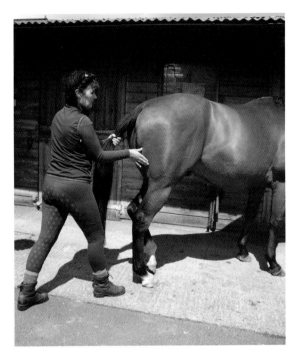

Thumbing down the hamstrings.

Dealing with Pain

Most horses who are tight in the semi-tendinosis and semi-membranosis feel the most discomfort as you come to the tendon at the bottom of the muscle, in line with the stifle. Therefore good observation of the horse's head and ears and awareness of his body tension as you approach this part is vital. As with the work on the Bladder channel, the key is not to be too hard or too fast. In some cases, it is necessary initially to simply lay the palm, or thumb, on the skin with absolutely no pressure and wait until the horse realises that you are not going to hurt him. Remember that they can feel a fly land and so even this may be enough for some.

For horses that cannot cope with any pressure on their hamstrings, even the lightest touch because the muscles are so tight and painful, there is another technique for loosening them where you do not even have to touch them! This technique will be shown in Chapter 8 (*see* Step 2: Rocking the Ribs).

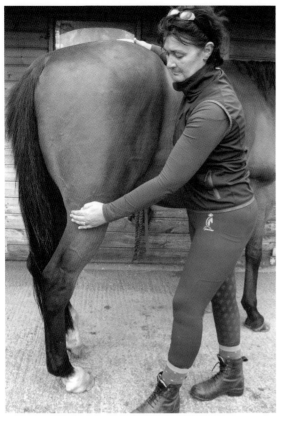

Releasing tension by laying the fingers on the tendon at the top of leg.

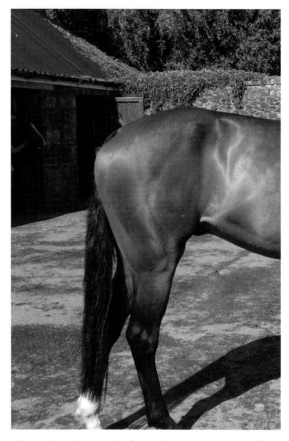

A horse showing tension from tuber coxae to point of hip.

Step 4: Tuber Coxae to Hip Joint

Tension in this area can occur for a variety of reasons but is commonly due to pain, past or present, lower down in the leg. It may be that the original problem has resolved but the horse has found a way of going that he knows is not painful and has simply remained like this until tension builds up here. Sometimes, the lines of stress are visible and easy to see but more often, you have to feel. If you run your thumb, fairly strongly up and down just behind the tuber coxae, you can then find the line, or lines, of tension.

Moving the Skin

If this area is very tight, the skin around the tuber coxae will feel as if it is glued down and so first, we need to gently get it moving. Using finger tips initially and then palms, move the skin in a circular motion around the tuber coxae until the skin moves freely. Make sure that you are moving the skin and not just the hair. If you find that it is just the hair that is moving, you need to allow your hands to stay still, with enough pressure to feel the softening of the fascia; then, while maintaining that amount of pressure, move the skin around slowly until it begins to move more easily.

Moving the skin around the tuber coxae.

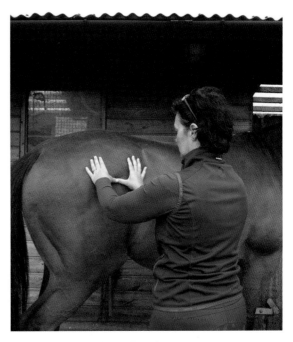

Thumb pressure behind the tuber coxae.

Working the Line of Tension

As most of the tension is found nearest to the joint, begin with static pressure just behind the tuber coxae by placing one hand on top of the other and gently leaning in, giving the horse chance to respond by leaning back into the pressure. When the horse wants to increase the pressure, you can increase it by moving to place one thumb on top of the other on the line of tension.

From there, you can keep one thumb just behind the tuber coxae and use the other thumb to work down to the hip joint. You can do this two or three times or simply just stay at either end of the tension line. Be guided by your horse. Similarly, some horses like you to move down the line quite slowly whereas others want a more definite and faster way of working. If the method you choose does not work as well as you would like, change to a different amount of pressure and rhythm.

Step 5: Leg Jiggle

Now that you have loosened off the musculature of the hindquarters, we can check how easily the skeletal structures move. This is best done when the horse is resting a leg but it is still possible when standing with all the weight on the leg. When the leg is resting it is easier to get movement and increase that range of motion.

With the horse's toe resting on the ground, take hold of the hock with your fingers and gently move from side to side. If the horse is happy, you can shake more vigorously and check movement in the joints higher up. You should be able to see movement in the stifle, up to the hip joint and even up as far as the tuber sacrale right at the top. Movement here is not profound but should be visible. If the horse allows, you can take hold of the stifle instead of the hock and move it from side to side, which makes it easier to see movement at the top. Please be careful, however, because if there is a problem within the stifle then the horse will not be happy with this technique. With this technique, you should also be able to see

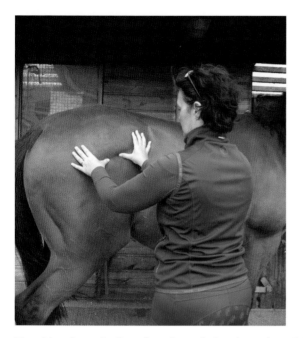 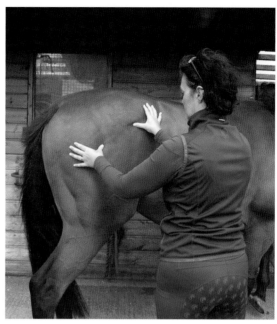

Thumbing down the line of tension to help release the pelvis.

movement all the way down the spine so that the head and neck will move. You can then say that you can get your horse's neck to shake from side to side by using only two fingers!

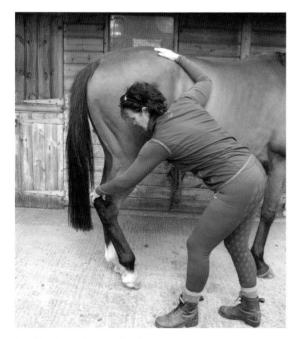 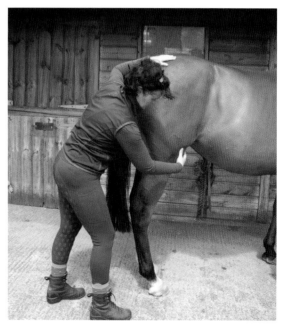

Leg jiggle – using the hock.

Leg jiggle – using the stifle.

CHAPTER 8

Opening the Shoulders and Ribcage

The Ribcage and Abdomen

The ribcage is an area of the horse that is often overlooked when it comes to looking at the overall picture, but when a horse is blocked through his ribs, the back cannot swing and it is also more difficult for him to use his core muscles. Sometimes, horses with this issue are reluctant to move and so a whip or spurs may be used on exactly the area that is uncomfortable already. Other horses will have the opposite reaction and rush off too fast. This can result in the application of strong bits or martingales. Not going forward or going forward too fast are two sides of the same coin and are often indicative of pain or discomfort. This is not limited to this area of the body but it is unfortunate when horses with sore sides then get more pressure put on that exact area.

Rushing through gates or doorways can be an indication of a problem in this area. It is possible that a door, or gate, has swung shut in the past but if you are careful about opening the stable door, or field gate, wide and the horse continues to rush through, have a look at their ribs. The explanation for this comes when you consider that in most circumstances, what happens after passing through the door or gate is that the horse is asked to turn 90 degrees very sharply; it is this action that causes the reaction but the horse associates the pain with the door or gate.

Step 1: Moving the Skin – Circles and Stretches

Circles

The skin should glide easily over the body but what you will find is that in some areas it will and in others it may feel as if it has been glued down. Remember that movement melts fascia and so gently getting the skin to move is the first step to freeing up the ribs and abdomen and reducing any restrictions. Place the hands side by side, with your fingers resting just over the top of the ribs, just behind the shoulder. You need enough pressure to get 'hold' of the skin. If things move easily, this will be very little pressure but if the skin is stuck to the body then a little more pressure will be required, or all you will move is hair. Slowly make a circular motion with both hands going in the same direction together. Try to use body movement to do this, which means primarily that your hips will rotate on a vertical plane and, by this action, your hands will do the same. If it sounds strange, try it without the horse to start.

Shiatsu without the Horse

Keeping your shoulders down and relaxed, raise your hands as if they were sitting on the horse's ribcage and move your hips in a clockwise direction. You will need to keep your legs hip-width apart so that, as you drop down on the circle, your body is able to stay upright and spinally aligned. It is worth mentioning that you should be able to do all of the techniques without the benefit of the horse to lean on. We call it 'Working the Invisible Horse'.

Having completed a few circles in one area, move the hands horizontally along to the next bit until you reach the end of the ribs. Then come back to behind the shoulder and drop down to the area below and continue. Keep going in this pattern until you have worked the whole side, including the belly. As you get lower down the horse's sides, you may have to use a wider stance in order to stay in a good position. Depending on the size of you and the size of your horse, you might find it easier to turn the hands over and work with the back of your hands on the horse as you move under the belly.

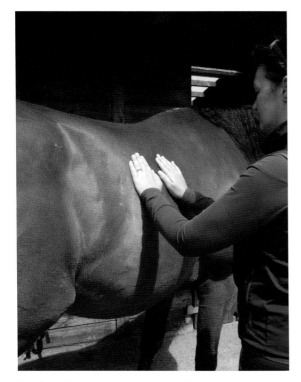

Moving skin over abdomen by moving both hands together in a circle.

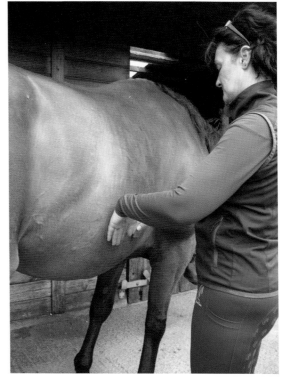

Moving skin on lower abdomen – hands inverted.

Working on Little Ones

For this technique and the following one, if you are working with something very small, such as a Shetland pony, it is sometimes easier to lean over the top and work the other side. This also has the advantage of often being safer. Due to their size, Shetlands have the possibilities of both biting and kicking at the same time. It is much more difficult to find a safe working position. However, if you are leaning over the top of them and you reach an area of discomfort that causes a reaction, they will turn to the side where your hands are, then you can both see them coming and have the chance to get out of the way if necessary.

Moving skin on a Shetland from the other side.

Stretching

If the skin is now all gliding smoothly over the ribs and abdomen, this next technique should be simple. Place your hands side by side but a few centimetres apart with the tips of your fingers just below the top of the ribs, in the middle of the back, and apply enough pressure to hold the skin by leaning your body in towards the horse. As you breathe out, move your hands apart, taking the skin with them and thereby creating a stretch between your hands. Move each hand a few more centimetres out and repeat until you reach either side of the ribs. Come back to centre, drop down by the length of your hands and repeat. Continue this process until the whole area has been stretched. Make sure that you are actually stretching the skin between your hands. You should be able to see the stretch quite easily. Try not to let your hands slide over the skin as then all you achieve is moving the hair. Loosening off all this area will make working on the shoulders and front legs much simpler.

Step 2: Rocking the Ribs

This is a truly fabulous technique as it works the whole horse and directly addresses so many different areas of possible tension. This is the technique mentioned in the previous chapter that loosens the hamstrings without touching them. It also helps release the deep iliopsoas muscles, again without touching them, which is useful because they are too deep for any palpation. It moves and releases all the back muscles and even the hindquarters and the neck. Because it can move so much, many horses are a little unsure of this for the first time. For some, a gentle, slow approach is useful the first few times, as it is worth it, to be able to do so much with so little effort. Once the horse accepts his ribs being rocked then this technique can be done two-handed, with one hand on top of the other, to create a more intense movement; initially, though, it is best to work with one supporting hand and one working hand. It may be that the horse is happy to accept two hands within a few minutes but some are not and

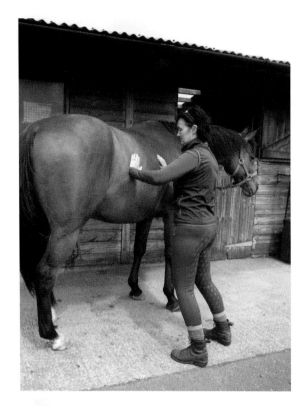

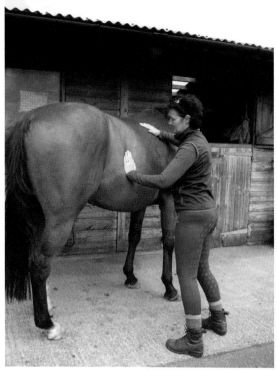

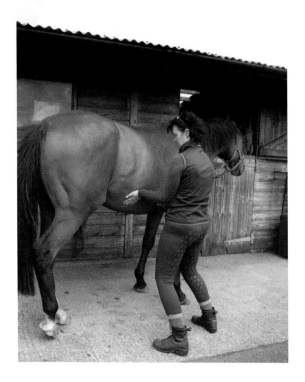

Lean in to stretch the skin over the abdomen as the hands move apart.

will step away to avoid what is happening. Horses that are particularly tense often find it difficult to comprehend , or accept, that a part of their body that is not being touched starts to move, as if on its own. Just go as slowly and as gently as you can, keeping contact with the supporting hand and, if possible, the working hand. If the horse moves away, stop for a minute until the horse stops moving and begin again at a point in the procedure that the horse is happy to accept.

Place the supporting hand behind the scapula, at the top of the ribs or wherever you feel comfortable. Lay the working hand beside it and gently work across the ribs, using the heel of your hand to bounce gently over the ribs. As you go, you can note if there are any ribs that appear to be higher than the others and check afterwards to see if this is still the situation. When you get to the edge of the ribs, continue bouncing down until you reach the bottom of the ribs. If you have a fat horse and cannot feel the ribs, make sure you know where they are because if you end up bouncing on the horse's intestines then he has good reason not to be happy.

If, or when, your horse is happy and accepting of this, you can place the supporting hand over the top of the working hand so that both of them are now bouncing the ribs. This is called a bouncing technique as it is akin to the feeling you get when bouncing a ball, with rhythm and lightness while getting faster as you proceed. Be careful to not just push but rather to create a swing in the ribcage. Stay bouncing until the back moves along its whole length, the neck and head start to move and there is as much movement through the side you are not working as there is on your side. It may take a few minutes for this to happen but even if it starts to happen quite quickly, keep working so that the movement can ripple out and in to affect the whole horse.

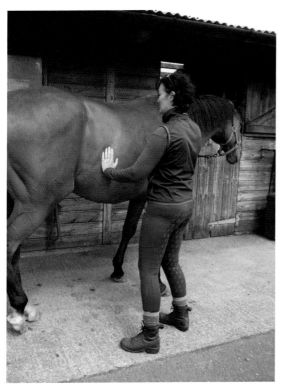

Rocking the ribs – place one hand behind the scapula while the other hand bounces the ribs.

Rocking the ribs – place one hand on top of the other and bounce with the heel of the hand.

You can check the state of the hamstrings using the Gentle, Safe Muscle Movement technique in Step 3 of Chapter 7. If you think that the hamstrings need to relax more, then keep bouncing. If the lumbar area was tight when you worked the Bladder channel and you want to help it relax some more, this technique will help for this too but is best followed up by the rearward hind leg stretch that is described in Chapter 9. This will help to stretch out the iliopsoas muscles. These are deep muscles that help to bring the hind leg forward and up. When a horse does not, or cannot, use the other muscles responsible for this movement, the iliopsoas muscles become overworked and tight, often showing as a raised area behind the saddle. As this is also a classic area for fat pads, it can be mistaken as simply fat but this is not always the case.

The Abdomen

While there are advanced techniques that can work on the internal organs of the body, they are, unfortunately, beyond the scope of this book. However, relaxing and liberating the ribcage and the abdominal muscles will improve systems such as the respiratory and digestive systems, which in turn help the circulatory system and therefore the immune system. In fact, all systems benefit from not just these techniques but the whole Shiatsu experience and that is why it is such a special therapy.

The Shoulders

Tension in the shoulders occurs for numerous reasons. Some of them, such as an ill-fitting saddle, can cause direct constriction in the shoulder. Others result as a knock-on from front leg lameness, especially if that problem is ongoing or not quickly resolved, such as navicular or laminitis. As mentioned in Chapter 2, over a hundred years ago, vets used to think that navicular was a shoulder problem. Nowadays, we know that it is a syndrome with a variety of different causes and so veterinary

attention is concentrated on the precise part that is causing the problem and there is little or no attention paid to the knock-on effects. However, if the horse has been trying to relieve pain in one part of his body, he will overuse another area to compensate and therefore, in many respects, navicular can be a shoulder problem.

There are also other reasons for shoulder tension, which vary from a problem further back, so that the horse is reluctant to power forward with his hind legs, such as if the horse has ulcers, or he is unable to power forwards due to injury in the hind end. There is also a direct connection between the head and the shoulders through the hyoid apparatus and so tension in the jaw and poll can also lead to tight shoulders.

Step 1: Say Hello

Many horses are sensitive around the back of the elbow and girth area and so rather than diving straight into the next step, take a few moments to simply move the skin over the outside of the shoulder. Usually, one hand is enough for this and the other hand can rest on the withers so you can observe the horse's face while you do this. If you feel that the muscles over, and behind, the scapula are tight and unyielding, a little percussion might be in order but if everything moves well then you can move on to Step 2. Immediately.

Step 2: Opening the Shoulder

Releasing the Back of the Shoulder

From the point of view of you, the giver, this method employs a mix of some of the strategies already covered in other techniques. Facing the head of the horse, point your outside leg forward, with feet pointing forward. Use the lunging position employed as we worked palming and fingering down the hamstrings in Step 3 in Chapter 7, so you can work down the back of the shoulder. Stand beside your horse and place the hand nearer to him on his withers. This is the supporting hand. You are not going to be trying to get underneath the scapula but rather imagine a line from the back edge of the scapula down to the elbow.

Place the working hand just behind the back edge of the scapula, flat on the skin with the fingers pointing upwards. With your outside leg forward, lean into your hand, giving the impression of trying to fold the skin behind the shoulder underneath the scapula. The muscle in front of your hand should produce a small wave motion. Come back out slowly and move down until you get level with the point of the shoulder. As you move in, remember to breathe out, and as you descend, sink your body lower to keep spinally aligned. Make sure that, in your effort to move the muscle, your body does not get in front of your hand. You cannot lean into your hand if it is further back than the rest of you!

When you get to a point level with point of shoulder, rotate your hand 180 degrees so that your fingers are now pointing to the ground and keep your thumb tucked in so that it too points downwards. Continue moving inwards behind the elbow and down until

you can go no further. This technique is lovely for keeping your hands warm in the winter but there are some things to consider. As with working the hamstrings, move in and out slowly. Give the horse time to consider what is happening as they may want to lean more weight into your pressure. If this occurs, you can jam your elbow against your own body to help support the weight of the horse. However, there may also be horses who do not appreciate this technique, so watch out for signals that you need to slow down and use less pressure.

Releasing the Front of the Shoulder

Unlike human beings, horses generally do not deliberately tense an area before you try to work it. Opening the front of the scapula is the exception, however, and so on some horses, this technique is very hard and requires a great deal of patience, as well as several sessions, but the result will be a much more comfortable horse.

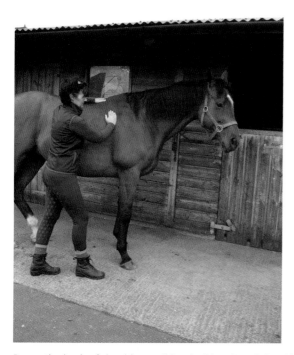 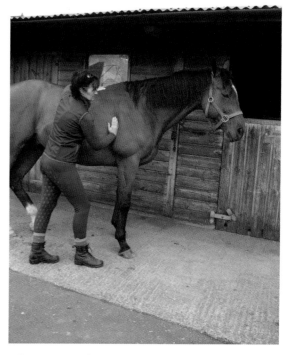

Down the back of shoulder until level with point of shoulder – leaning in as if to move the skin from the ribcage under the shoulder.

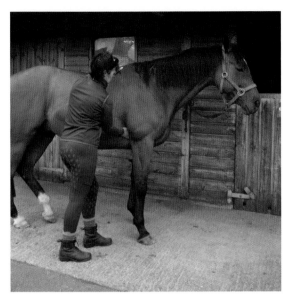

Down the back of the shoulder – rotating the hand so the fingers point downwards.

Perseverance and Patience

Many years ago, I went to a demonstration by someone who had basically borrowed several ideas from different therapies. When he opened the front of the shoulder, it was, in my opinion, positively brutal, but the relief that it gave the horse was very obvious. Having seen this I decided that, while I would never want to be anywhere as forceful, it was worthwhile persevering for longer in opening the front of the shoulder and patience is the order of the day. The other side of the story is that I once used to work with a horse that could do Spanish walk and you could lose your whole hand down behind the scapula.

Begin by stroking down just in front of the scapula, to help the horse relax and to make sure that you are in the right place. In horses that are very tight here, the definition between bone and soft tissue is not always easy to feel and, sometimes, beginners find themselves trying to move into the bone and not around it. The scapula is a big bone and is quite thick so it is not simply a case of folding the skin over itself.

The angle of direction of pressure is important. If you try to use the outside edge of your hand, it may be too thick and if we use the fingers, it may be uncomfortable for the horse, unless you have very short nails and even then, it is not the ideal approach. Therefore, you need to hold your hand at an approximately 45-degree angle to the edge of the scapula, so that your little finger will be the first point of contact. Think of the angle of a knife cutting into a cake.

Stand facing the horse's head, place the hand nearer to the horse on the withers and begin at the top of the scapula, working your way down. For the first third or so of the neck, there will be little indentation but after that you should be able to get in behind the bone. Once you have managed this, the supporting hand moves to join the working hand, just above it, so that now both hands can be in behind the scapula. The job of the supporting hand is to try to hold on to the position should the other hand slip out due to the horse moving or stretching. If the horse stretches away from you then you can easily lose the connection, but the horse is actively trying to help, so do not make him bring his head back simply because you are not finished. If you can encourage the horse to bring his head and neck down and towards you, it will help the muscles to relax and make it easier to do.

If the horse is really relaxed, you may be able to just slide your hands down and over the point of the shoulder but the number of horses that can do this at first are in the minority. So, release the pressure on the working hand enough to move down while still maintaining the ability to stay under the bone and slide down a few centimetres and lean in again. This may be where patience is required as often the horse has to think about what is happening and then the muscle will just relax. Because your pressure is static and therefore constant, we are looking to interrupt the message from the brain that is telling the muscle to be tight, and if it can do it once, it can do it again.

You may have to change your body position to be able to lean in directly but this will depend on the size of the horse and how tight he is.

Each time you move the working hand and successfully relax that part, move the supporting hand down to join it. The most difficult part to release is often at point of shoulder where the brachiocephalicus and the sternocephalicus can be found. If it is absolutely impossible to release this area with your fingers then gently place one thumb on the tightest part and wait until you feel the tension start to melt under it. This may not release very much initially but it is a small change and sometimes that is what we need to aid the whole process. Added to which, if these muscles are tight here, there will also be tension at the other end, by the top of the head, and we have yet to address anything here, unless you decided to work the head beforehand.

Working the Chest

There are several interesting energy channels over the chest and if you follow your intuition you will fall into the place where the horse needs you to be. For some horses, this will be just to the inside of the humerus, but in others you will find your fingers in the middle of the descending pectoral muscles. The technique used here is similar to working down the hindquarters of the Bladder channel. Stand facing the head, place the supporting hand on the top of the withers, cup the chest in line with point of shoulder with your other hand and lean backwards to apply pressure, all the while remembering to breathe. Come up to move the hand down and repeat until you reach the top of the horse's leg.

Joining the Back and the Front – Does a Horse Have 'Armpits'?

The short answer is 'yes, he does' but despite searching all the anatomy books I can find, I cannot find a name for them. Basically, however, you are looking to release the pectoral muscles, in particular the transverse pectoral muscle, which in turn will relax the sternum and everything that attaches to it. Horses that are tight in this area generally do not breathe properly as everything is constricted, and so releasing this part of the horse will bring many benefits.

Stand facing your horse's shoulder and place your hands on either side of the top of the inside of the leg. You should be able to feel the body against the edge of your index finger. Do not try to make the fingers of each hand meet unless that is very easy. Using body movement, lift up and into the 'armpit'. Work in gradually until the fingers meet. You should be able to feel the horse's ribs against your knuckles. Please be aware that, occasionally, the horse will close his elbows to increase the pressure and you might feel that your fingers are totally squashed. The horse obviously wants this and so do your best to stay as long as you can, or until you are released!

Step 3: Moving the Whole Thoracic Sling

This technique is best done when both shoulders have been opened. Having released the shoulders, it should be possible for the whole of the thoracic sling to move freely as there are no bones holding it steady, as in a human being. The ability to do this needs interaction with the abdominal muscles and the back needs to be able to flex. This is a useful exercise for horses who have forgotten that they can do this.

Stand facing the tail and place the flat of your hand on the sternum. You will feel movement through your hand so the area to watch is the thoracic part of the trapezius muscle and possibly the whole of the back. Using the same angle that the scapula forms, lift the sternum as if to the withers. The correct angle is important as you will not get movement if you just try to lift upwards. Having lifted, you can simply relax and the thoracic sling will generally fall back of its own accord, especially if the horse finds this difficult.

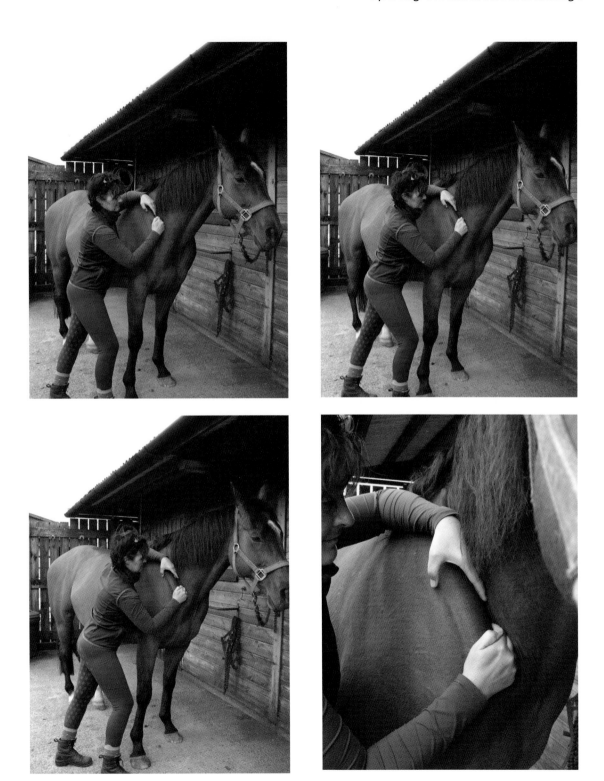

Releasing the front of the shoulder by opening up the scapula.

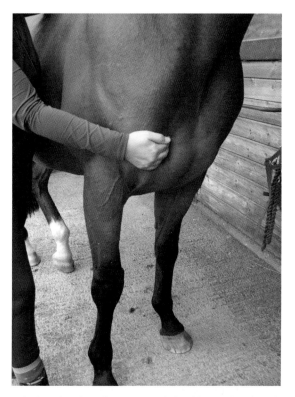

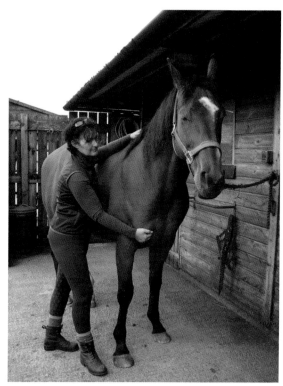

Relaxing the chest from point of shoulder to the top of the leg.

Lifting the hands upwards to open the space between
the ribcage and the front leg.

 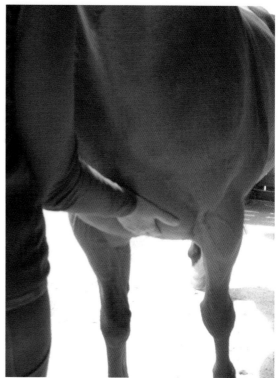

Pushing the sternum up in the same angle as the scapula to release the thoracic sling.

CHAPTER 9

Leg Rotations and Stretches

Leg rotations and stretches are both ways of moving Ki. Obviously, you are also moving muscles, tendons, ligaments and joints but we need to think of this in terms of moving Ki, first and foremost. What this means is that it is not vital, or necessary, to make the rotations a certain size or the stretches more than the horse is willing to offer. What we are trying to do is to take the legs, in this case, to a point of tension and if the horse feels relaxed and confident that he can do more, then we support him through this. Then we know that the Ki has moved. There should never be any force involved in these procedures as that can cause physical damage and pain.

At which point in the session that leg rotations and stretches are asked for can vary from horse to horse. Sometimes, it is a good idea to perform these after opening and relaxing the area to which the leg in question is attached. For example, you could do the techniques found in Chapter 7 and immediately follow up with hind leg rotations and stretches. Alternatively, you might like to open the whole of the body and then do all four leg rotations and stretches. At that point, you need to decide whether working with the hind legs first or the front legs first is most appropriate. Whatever you choose, make sure that you do both hind legs or both front legs together. If your horse has difficulty lifting his abdomen and bringing the hind legs under him, waiting until the shoulders and ribcage have been worked may make this easier; then you can ask for a front leg stretch,

which will engage the back muscles. However, it may be that the shoulders have been so tight that working with the front legs first will make things easier. It all depends!

As the front legs are easier to rotate and stretch, we shall begin there. It is important to state that there are many different front leg stretches that can be done but, for now, we will limit this to the most common and the stretches that achieve the most for the beginner.

Front Leg Rotations

If you have left the rotations and stretches to nearer the end of your session then we need to 'wake' things up again before going into the rotation. Even if you do this immediately after opening the shoulder and thoracic sling, however, this next technique is a useful one because it does so much.

Front Leg Jiggle

Stand facing the rear of the horse, keep your outside leg a step forward from your inside leg and maintain a wide base by keeping your feet at least hip-width apart. Pick up the front leg using the inside hand nearer the horse, holding the pastern. As you turn to face the horse, transfer the holding of the pastern to the other hand and squat down so that you can rest the elbow of what was your outside hand on your knee. With the other hand, take hold of the horse's leg just above the knee and with this hand only, shake the leg back and forwards towards you. This should cause the muscles in the shoulder to move and ripple and as you increase the movement, the ripples will extend in the middle and along the back. This technique will work most of the horse and so it can be used on its own at any time. It can be used as a pre-ride technique if you are too short of time to do much more, as well as a precursor to the leg rotations.

Front Leg Rotations

This is a dance. Your dancing partner is the horse's leg and so you must move together as one. Although we call this a leg rotation, in effect it is more about the shoulder, but having loosened the shoulder off, it should be easier for the horse.

Step 1

Turn back so that you are facing the rear, keep your outside hand holding the pastern and, with your shoulder resting against the horse's shoulder, bring your other hand around the inside of the leg to hold it just below the knee.

Step 2

Holding the leg close so that the forearm rests against your thigh, slowly rotate your hips and whole body on a horizontal plane, so that the leg moves with you. It should seem as if you were drawing circles with the horse's knee, which ideally should be pointing to the ground. Horses who are tight through the front edge of the shoulder will hold their leg more forward but this does not matter. The centre of this circle as if drawn by the knee should be over where the horse

would stand. When the leg is forward, the knee points to a position that is also further forward and so often the tensions in the rear of the shoulder are bypassed. Initially, however, this is not something to try to correct but rather to note and hope that you see an improvement with over time.

The circles should be quite small to start with, gradually increasing in size while decreasing in speed. It is preferable to make smaller circles that are round than angular shapes that are bigger. If your horse has been using his forehand more than he should then moving the leg back could be more problematic as the muscles behind the shoulder have become overdeveloped and blocked. Also, this action causes the scapula to move back and the horse needs to be able to lift his shoulders and ribcage to let the back extend.

There are some horses who seem to have forgotten that their legs can move out and in, as well as back and forward. By using your body to move the leg and shoulder, you can feel where the horse feels most reluctant and slow down to allow him to relax into the rotation so that it gets easier with each circle. How many rotations you need to do will depend on the horse but generally four to six should be more than enough. Be careful about how long you are asking the horse to stand on three legs if he is young, old or has any issues that may mean this is difficult for him.

Front Leg Stretches

There are many different stretches and many different ways of doing them. For the purposes of this book, however, we will try to use the simplest way of doing them and show three different front leg stretches, namely forward, down and sideways.

Forward Front Leg Stretch

The reason for choosing the method of forward stretch shown here is because it helps prevent back

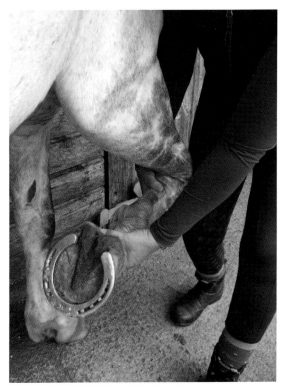

In position for front leg rotation.

strain for the giver and it makes it easier to deal with horses that want to lean on you and give you all their weight. However, the following method of doing a forward front leg stretch is not suitable for very small ponies or miniature horses; because of their size, a forward leg stretch is better done in the same manner as the forward hind leg stretch, which will be described later in this chapter.

Getting into Position

You, or your horse, might want to put the leg down for a minute after the rotations but it is not absolutely necessary. You can simply get into position and take the leg with you. Stand in front of the horse with your legs hip-width apart so that you have one knee pointing at either side of the leg. If you have put the leg down, pick it up by asking the

horse to bend his knee and hold it just above the knee. You can, at this stage, lift the leg higher to stretch out the pectoral muscles and then relax. When you have the leg in a comfortable position for the horse, take one hand and bring the lower leg so that you can close your knees and hold the leg in position. Normally, your legs will hold him just below his knee but it will depend on the size of you and the size of your horse. It is important to keep the feet apart but pointed inwards. This will enable you to keep hold of the horse's leg and walk back and forward, if the horse is unsure about stretching. If you have a lighter horse, you should be able to hold his leg between yours without using your hands, but a heavier horse will require more support and you can cup both hands under his forearm. However, try to make sure that you do not collapse through your diaphragm, and are not using muscular strength to hold his leg, because

Four corners of the circle from front leg rotation.

then you cannot breathe, or see what is happening in the rest of the horse, while stretching.

The Stretch

The stretch is done by the horse and not by you. No force is used to make stretches. Simply lean back slightly and allow the horse to stretch forward. Ideally, we are looking for a stretch that comes all the way from the sacroiliac joint so that it means the back stretches too. Sometimes, the horse will lean back to make the stretch like a cat and this means that he is stretching out his shoulders but avoiding the back being stretched. If this happens the first few times only, then this is not a problem. At least he is stretching something and he knows what he needs to stretch. It may be that he needs to free up the shoulders a bit more before engaging the rest of his body or that he just does not feel secure and confident enough to release everything initially. However, if you feel that he is really not happy with the idea of stretching through the back then perhaps there is something that needs a more professional evaluation.

You might also find that your horse starts stretching his neck away from you at this point. This is good and one of the reasons why we do not want the horse to be tightly restrained when working – so that even if you have had to tie him, he needs the room to be able to stretch like this. Notice if your horse positions himself near to the wall when you are doing this as many horses look as if they want to stretch their necks to the side but find they cannot because of the wall. Do not be fooled – the horse knows exactly what is going on and has found a way not to stretch. This is interesting to note because we can be aware of this when we start neck stretches as shown in the next chapter.

The Downward Front Leg Stretch

This stretch will help to release the thoracic sling and tension in the trapezius muscles. Naturally, it will affect all the soft tissue around the shoulder because everything is connected but it is particularly useful for horses who are blocked through the withers.

Getting into Position

For this one, you will need to take more care in order to prevent being stood on or bowled over, so please be careful and be aware of where you are and what your horse is doing. Once again, stand in front of the horse but this time your whole body needs to be just to the outside so that if the horse steps forward, he steps past you and not on, or over, you. Your outside leg is forward and then you can pick up the horse's leg using your outside hand under the forearm; as the horse lifts his leg, sink down until you are squatting beside him, with your other hand around the pastern.

The Stretch

The leg needs to be at an angle of no more than the angle of the scapula because you are asking the whole

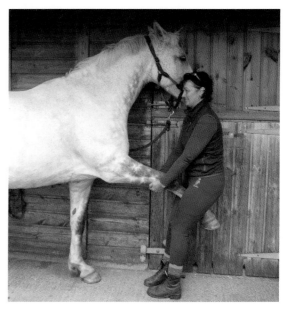

Front leg stretches with support.

Front leg stretch without support.

Front leg stretch with collapsed diaphragm.

How to Beat Avoidance Tactics

It is possibly not fair to call these avoidance tactics as, generally, it tends to be more of a confidence issue. The horse wants to stretch but is worried about it. There are two main ways of avoiding the stretch. One is leaning forward and the other is pawing, where the leg is pulled back and then thrown forward continuously.

To Prevent Leaning

Assuming your horse is healthy enough to stand on his three legs easily, there is no need for him to give you all his weight. If he is only leaning on you slightly, you may be able to push him back with one hand on his chest to take his own weight. Alternatively, if he is trying to give you it all, you can bend in half at the waist and put your shoulder against his chest. You need to be able to keep your back straight in order to prevent getting hurt and also this will still enable you to breathe. You may need to stand closer to the horse to achieve this.

To Alleviate Pawing

This usually happens when the horse is tight behind the shoulder and, as his leg comes forward, he feels the restriction and pulls back. Ultimately, he knows he needs to stretch, but cannot work out how. First, we need to take the flying leg out of the equation to prevent injury to you primarily, and so we fold the leg in half in a neutral position where the horse is comfortable. Take the leg just above the knee with the hand nearer to the horse, take hold of the pastern with the other hand and bend the leg in half so that both come together. Place the horse's knee against your body to secure it. This can often fit quite nicely into your hip. The leg is now no longer flying wildly and this makes things much safer. From our neutral position, lean back very slightly so that you can see the skin behind the shoulder and then immediately relax back into neutral.

Continue doing this while gradually increasing the stretch until you feel you have released the shoulder and ribcage to the point that the leg can become part of the stretch once again. If you have done enough then the leg simply needs to be extended to full length and be held between your thighs. While the horse works out what is happening, he may pull back a little and then stretch, and so it is at this point that you need to be able to walk forwards and then back as he gets used to the idea of being able to stretch.

Preventing leaning.

Preventing pawing.

leg and shoulder to drop down. If you cannot see the top of the shoulder from this position, keep an eye on the elbow and it will drop as the horse releases. Do not pull, but give some gentle traction in the direction in which you want the horse to stretch. They often let go quite quickly but if it takes you

by surprise, the worst that will happen is the hoof will hit the ground. However, you need to make sure that the hoof drops because the shoulder is released and not because they have walked forward. This is why you need to see the elbow – if they have just walked forward, then there will be no drop of the elbow. You should feel a decisive drop. If the horse refuses to let go, try lessening the angle of the leg so that it becomes just off the vertical. If this still does not make something happen, you can try the next stretch first and then try again.

The Sideways Front Leg Stretch

This stretch involves the shoulder and the ribcage and is useful for horses that struggle to bend and to wake up the soft tissues at the front end that are needed for lateral work.

Getting into Position

Stand in front of the horse as in the previous stretch and pick up the leg. The height at which the leg is held will depend on what part of the horse you are looking to stretch. The lower the hoof is to the ground, the higher the bit on the horse that will be stretched. In effect, if the hoof is close to the ground then the withers will stretch and if the leg is parallel to the ground then the abdominal muscles will be stretched. However, to stretch the ribcage, the leg needs to be approximately halfway between the two.

The Stretch

With the hand closer to the horse, support the fetlock and with the other hand, hold the leg above the horse's knee. Place the leg against your thigh and lean in towards the horse, taking the leg across the body so that you can see a stretch along the whole side of the horse. How far you have to lean in will depend on each individual horse.

Position for downward front leg stretch.

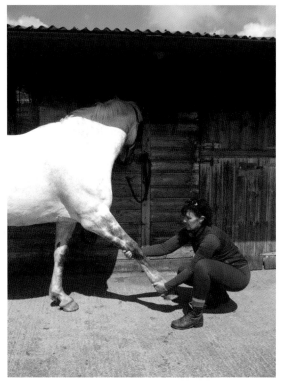

Down stretch.

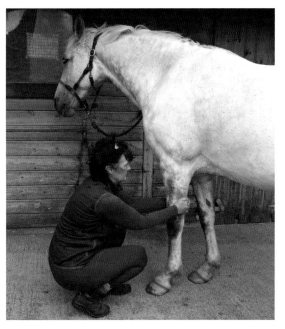

Shaking the front leg back and forwards can be useful for horses that are unable to lift their legs to stretch.

Hind Leg Rotations

Hind Leg Jiggle

As with the front legs, you might like to 'wake up' the legs with a jiggle as described in Step 5 in Chapter 7. This will shake out the muscles as well as gently loosen the joints before beginning the rotations.

Hind Leg Rotations

As with the front legs, this is a dance and while it is called a leg rotation, it is really more concerned with moving the hips. Tension in the hips and the lumbar area cause the most restrictions to this technique but if you have already loosened off the hindquarters then it should be easier for the horse.

Position for side stretch.

Side stretch.

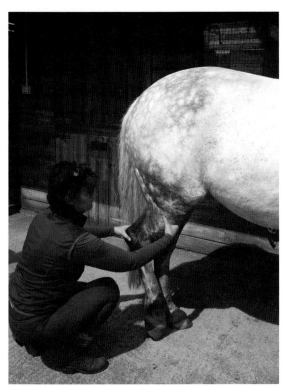

Hind leg jiggle.

Hind leg rotations – getting in position.

Step 1

With your outside leg forward, and with a wide stance, keep your shoulder against the hindquarters and pick up the hind leg. Wrap your inside arm around the front of the leg to hold it just below the hock. The upper part of the leg should now be resting on your forearm. The other hand holds and supports the pastern. Try to keep the hoof close to the ground with the toe relaxed and pointing downwards. To give an idea of how high the leg should be, imagine that if you have a shavings bed, the toe could draw a circle in the top of the shavings.

Step 2

You should now have the leg wrapped in your arms and close to your body. Slowly rotate your hips on a horizontal plane so that the whole leg rotates with you. Use your body movement and weight to create the movement; it will also help you to identify parts of the circle that are difficult for the horse to move through. Move more slowly through these areas until the movement is free and easy. As with the front legs, the circles need to start small and gradually increase but as they get bigger, so the movement needs to be slower. From here, it is relatively simple to move directly into the hind leg backward stretch.

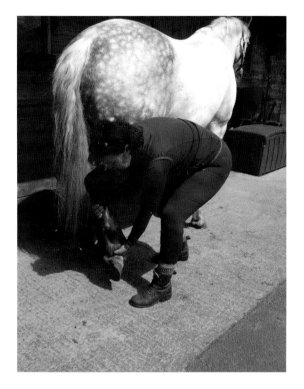

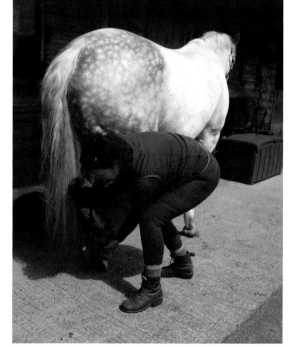

Hind leg rotations.

Hind Leg Stretches

For the purposes of this book, we will look at two hind leg stretches, forward and backward. The backward stretch will affect the lumbar area and the iliopsoas group as well as the abdominal muscles on the body, and then primarily, the muscles running down the front of the leg and the horse can often do this stretch of his own accord. The forward hind leg stretch is probably the most difficult one for the horse, and also for you. When the leg is stretched forward, it engages the muscles that the horse needs to use correctly when ridden, all along the back as well as the major muscles of the hindquarters. For this to work correctly, the shoulders will also have to lift and so this is why, sometimes, the shoulders need to be loosened off before a good stretch can be achieved.

The Backward Hind Leg Stretch

Getting in Position

If you have successfully managed to do hind leg rotations, then you are already in position. Make sure that your outside leg is far enough forward of your body so that if the horse goes for a big stretch, you can go with him and support him.

The Stretch

Lean your whole body forward, taking the leg with you. Do not push the leg away from you but go into the stretch as one smooth movement. Because you are using your body to move the leg, and not your arms, it is easier to feel exactly where the point of resistance occurs. When you feel that this stretch is enough for the horse, which might not necessarily be what you think he should be able to stretch, stop and wait for a moment. At this point, some horses may lean their whole body forward, thus enhancing the stretch. For others, you may just need to wait

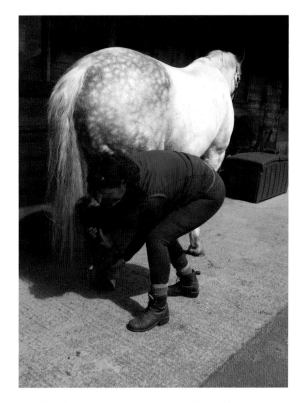

Hind leg backward stretch – getting in position.

a moment and then lean forward a bit more and increase the stretch. Take it slowly and try not to go beyond the point of tension. The idea is to gradually increase that point of tension so that the horse is comfortable and does not do himself any damage by overstretching.

The Forward Hind Leg Stretch

It is possible to move directly from one stretch to the next but initially many people find it easier to put the horse's foot back down and start again. The situation where this might not be the case is when you have a horse that is reluctant to pick up his foot; once you have got it up, you might like it to stay that way. If this is what you want to do then you need to be able to walk backwards to get your feet in the correct place,

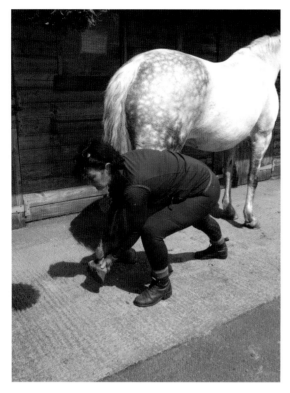

Hind leg backward stretch.

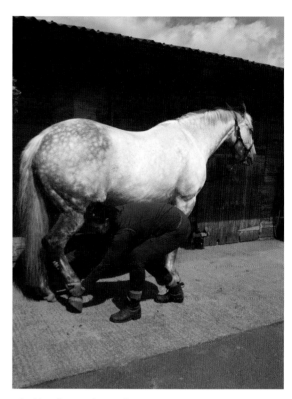

Hind leg forward stretch – getting in position.

while changing your hand positions to facilitate the next stretch. This requires you to be confident of where you need to be and how you need to change over, and a flexible, patient horse is required while you work it all out. Therefore, for now, we will put the foot down and start again.

Getting in Position

This part is very important for you as well as for the horse. If you are not in the correct position, you may not be able to support the horse and he will lose confidence in you, especially if he is concerned about this technique; you also need to take care for your own back as being in the wrong place can hurt you too.

Stand just behind, or beside, the front legs, facing the leg you are about to stretch. Where exactly you need to stand will depend on the size of you and the

size of the horse. However, please note that if the horse can perform this stretch well, his hind hoof will come almost to his front one and if you stand too close to the hind leg and he does a big stretch, you will either have to twist or you may drop him. Take as big a step forward with your outside leg as necessary to be able to bend down and pick up the horse's leg. Place your inside hand under the fetlock and your outside hand supporting just below the hock.

The Stretch

Pick up the leg and bring it towards you as you lean back and down until you are squatting beside the horse. As with front leg stretches, when you reach a point of tension, stop and wait for a moment. At this stage, some horses may lean back. Please do not think that this is avoidance; rather it is increasing the stretch down the semi-membranosis and semi-tendinosis. Other horses need a moment before stretching into your hold, engaging the back and abdominals. When the horse tells you he has had enough, place the leg back down on the ground.

Take note that breeds such as Arabs, Quarter Horses and thoroughbreds often only need small stretches, but they must hold them for several seconds and not give an instant snatch-like stretch. Once the Ki has moved, these horses' own extravagance of movement will allow them to work out how to move, and so it is better that they do smaller stretches for longer so that you can be sure that the message has reached the brain.

Hind leg forward stretch.

How to Beat Avoidance Tactics

There are two methods horses most commonly employ to avoid the forward hind leg stretch. The first is holding the leg up high and refusing to relax and the second is the hind leg version of the pawing described when talking about the front leg avoidance tactics. This can be that the horse is unsure and starts to take his leg forward and then takes it back and repeats this in a hesitant, but gentle, manner or it can sometimes be more of a wild thrashing. Obviously, the latter is potentially more dangerous and you need to be sure that you feel safe and in the right place to continue.

To Aid Relaxation of a Leg Held High

Do not try to pull the leg either forward or down. The horse is much stronger than you and this is a battle you cannot win. Instead, let the horse keep his leg where he wants and slowly and gently shake it. As you feel a relaxation, allow the leg to drop downwards, without coming forward. The first priority must be to get the horse confident enough to hold the leg in a relaxed manner, even if this means that he may only be stretching the distance of half a walking stride. Once the leg is relaxed, you may then be able to guide it to come more forward. This is much more likely to be achieved if you are now in the squat-down position as it will lower your energy, which in turn will encourage the horse to do likewise. Because your outside leg is forward, you should be able to stand up quite easily if the horse takes his leg back and you have to start again.

To Alleviate Snatching

In this situation, you will almost certainly have to stand and squat on a repeated basis as you try to maintain hold of the leg. Once again, make sure that you do not pull the leg forward but do ensure that you have a firm hold as the horse needs to have confidence that you will not drop him, if and when he decides to let go. Holding the leg below the hock and around the pastern helps to make the horse more confident about this. Ask for less of a stretch until the horse is comfortable and then allow him to stretch himself. It helps to speak reassuringly to encourage the horse. This will also ensure that you keep breathing, as you cannot speak without breathing.

CHAPTER **10**

Relaxing the Neck, Head and Tail

Relaxing the Neck

There are a great many techniques that can be used on the neck and so here we will discuss the simplest and most effective. There is a mix of muscle and ligament relaxing and softening, and stretches. Together, these can often realign any cervical vertebrae without the use of any force, or even meaningful pressure. So if your horse stretches, either of his own accord or because you have asked him for it, and there is a loud crack, do not worry; it is simply something putting itself back where is should be.

The neck stretches that we are looking for are to stretch forward, preferably from all the way along the back, a correct bend to the left and one to the right. We do not need the commonly used carrot stretches where the horse bends in two but rather a bend that you would ask for while riding. However, it must also have the horse's head perpendicular and not tilted. Sometimes a horse finds it difficult to stretch because he is tight in the withers or back, or in the poll and jaw. Poll tension and jaw tension tend to occur together and this will be discussed more fully later in this chapter. If you are struggling to get your horse to stretch forward, it might be a good idea to check out whether you need to work either end of the neck first.

Step 1: Jiggling the Neck

Place both hands side by side over the crest, just in front of the withers, and move each hand back and forward in opposite directions until the neck feels loose. Move up the neck in incremental measures until you reach the poll. For many horses, this is quite relaxing but if you have a very head-shy horse, just go as far as you can and move on to Step 2. Horses that are tight in this area feel as if there is an iron bar under your hands that does not want to do anything but remain as a fixed unit. These horses will find it difficult to stretch forward correctly.

Step 2: Percussion

Using your chosen method of percussion, begin at the bottom end of the neck and gently percuss the muscle, taking care not to percuss the bones. Advance up the neck in a manner that your horse finds acceptable and is happy for you to continue with. Do not be afraid to increase the pressure and speed if your horse agrees. However, if your horse is unhappy or worried, you can try an advance-and-retreat method: start just in front of the withers and begin your percussion, advance up the neck until

Jiggling the neck.

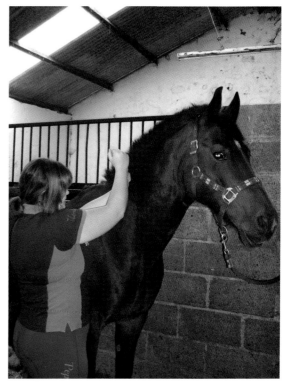

Percussion.

the horse shows that he is beginning to stress and, from there, move a few centimetres up the neck and immediately work back down to where you were. As your horse allows, gradually try to move further up the neck each time. Using this method, it is truly amazing how many head-shy horses really enjoy being pummelled to the top of the neck!

Step 3: Lifting the Nuchal Ligament

Once again, we begin at the bottom of the neck, in front of the withers. With both hands side by side on the top of the neck, take hold of the base of the mane and lift straight upwards. You should see the skin on the neck move with you. Continue in this way up the neck until you reach the head. If your horse refuses to allow this then there is a different way of working that does not have the same effect on the ligament

but will be a start so that you may be able to do this in the future.

Beginning in the same way, but without taking hold of the mane in a good handful, simply lift a few mane hairs so that they point straight up vertically. You can hold the hair near the crest and just slide your fingers along them in an upward direction. This very simple, but very gentle, technique will work to help the horse relax in a way that you will probably not believe while reading this!

Step 4: Incremental Forward Stretches

Take hold of the neck as in Step 1 and, if required, you can repeat this step but once you have moved the muscle, stretch the two hands apart. Work up the neck, stretching a few centimetres at a time until the whole neck is stretched. Then repeat the whole process

Lifting the nuchal ligament.

but have your hands further apart so that the stretch covers a greater part of the neck. Once you get to only two or three stretches to take in the whole neck, you can move on to the wither stretch, described in Step 5.

Step 5: Wither Stretch

Stand facing the horse and if the horse is happy for you to do so, place one hand on the top of the neck, in front of the withers, and the other under his chin, if he is happy to let you do so. This stretch is designed to connect the back and the neck by stretching the skin over the withers and, theoretically, the back muscles should stretch as well. Some horses will then want to continue stretching their necks out too, so having a hand under the chin allows you to support this. However, if they do not accept this hold then they are perfectly capable of doing this on their own. To facilitate the stretch over the withers, simply lean sideways or you can turn to face the tail and lean backwards, taking the skin with you.

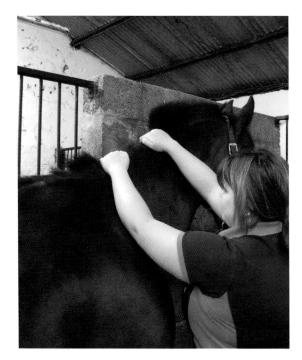

Incremental stretch.

Joining smaller incremental stretches together.

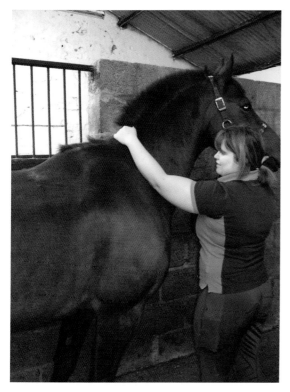

Wither stretch.

Neck Stretches

Forward Neck Stretch

Ideally, the stretch should be long and low so that there is stretch all the way from the hindquarters right out to the tip of the horse's nose. Having hopefully achieved a good stretch over the withers, you can simply move your working hand further up the neck and lean your body to produce the stretch, thereby incorporating more of the neck each time that you move until you reach the very top of the neck. When this works well, it is a simple and easy procedure that the horse will enjoy and appreciate. However, there are many reasons why a horse may be reluctant to comply and you might need to break down the stretch into even more parts.

To Help the Reluctant Horse

If you have a horse that is blocked, or believes he is blocked, at the withers, he will want to put his head up in the air while stretching. In order to ascertain that it is indeed the withers, and only the withers, that are truly blocked, allow him to put his head up, place your hands on either side of the jaw from underneath and lean forward. If he wants to walk forward to evade the stretch, put your bottom against his chest to prevent him from doing this. Many horses that are blocked through the withers also have tension in the poll and jaw area, but if you can persuade him to open up this part into a stretch, even if it is only part of what you are looking for, then it means you are at least halfway there. You can then return to Step 5: Wither Stretch and concentrate a little more on that technique.

If, on the other hand, the blockage is at the head end of the neck, it would be useful to try some of the techniques that will be mentioned later in this chapter.

Knowing When to Stop

If you have been following the techniques more or less as set out so far, you will not have done the majority, or maybe any, of the head and tail work and it is always tempting to make sure that you do everything. However, if you have a horse that is quite tight through his topline, or shows either of the tension mentioned previously (at the withers or the head end of the neck), and you then get a really fabulous stretch from the nose to the tail, it can be an idea to stop at that point. You then finish on a good note, with the horse feeling content and needing time to process this and consider the sensations within his body. Knowing when to stop is just as important as anything else concerned with Equine Shiatsu.

Side Neck Stretches

There are a great many different ways to do side neck stretches and it is best that we begin with the stretch that is the simplest one for horses that struggle to achieve a good bend of the neck. The object is simply to get a gentle curve of the neck with the head remaining perpendicular and not being allowed to tilt to the side. By this time in the session, you should know in which direction your horse prefers to bend, or alternatively, to which side he can bend more correctly. It is to this direction you must first ask your horse to bend.

Moving the Neck Away from You

This method of bending the neck allows for not only creating the correct curve of the neck but also helps prevent the head from tilting to the side, keeping it upright and perpendicular.

Getting into Position

First, stand on the opposite side of the neck from which you want it to bend so that the neck will move away from you. Place one hand on the side of the horse's head. Usually, placing it just beside the eye will be satisfactory but for some horses, it will need to be higher and closer to the ear. The more the horse wants to tilt his head, the higher you will need to place your hand. The other hand comes from under the neck and is laid at the top of the neck, with your palm facing towards you. Once more, make sure that you have a wide enough stance and be prepared to move your feet in order to stay with the horse. Do not plant your feet and try to do this technique with the force of your hands and arms.

Step 1

Gently push the hand on the head away from you while bringing the hand on the neck towards you. The hand on the head keeps it upright and the hand on the neck creates the bend. Your focus needs to be on the hand that is on the neck and you need your body to follow this one and not the hand on the head.

Step 2

Relax your pressure and, if the horse is very tight, he will automatically move back into the straight position. Move your hand down the neck slightly and repeat. Repeat Steps 1 and 2 until you reach the bottom of the neck. Because your body needs to follow the hand on the neck, you should find that you have turned away from the head and should be facing the opposite shoulder by the end.

Step 3

Return to the starting position and work down the neck while moving the head away from you, this time omitting Step 2 and so creating a smooth, gentle turn of the neck. You need only make a turn as far as needed for turning a corner and not bend the neck in half or allow the horse to twist his head right around. Sometimes the horse will do this in order to avoid the stretch you are looking for.

Bringing the Neck Towards You

This technique will allow you to have greater control over the bend in the neck but it is much easier for a horse to tilt his head and avoid keeping his head upright. There are many ways of achieving this stretch and much will depend on the size of you and the size of the horse. It is all about giving the horse something to bend around. This can be your hand, your shoulder or, if they are little, your hip.

Getting into Position

This time you will be bringing the neck towards you and so you need to be on the same side as the

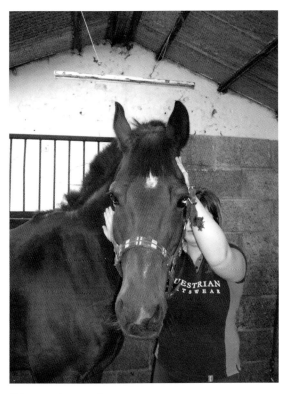

Side stretch away from you.

stretch, facing the neck. Place one hand at the top of the neck and wrap the fingers of your other hand around the nose, making sure that it is high enough not to restrict the horse's breathing.

Step 1

Lean in gently to the hand on the neck while asking the horse to bring his head towards you. Take care not to push the horse away from you but rather just give him support to bend around. Relax and allow the head to go back to centre. Move the hand on the neck down a little towards you and repeat until you reach the bottom of the neck. Once again, try to make a bend similar to that which you would want while riding and do not allow the horse to turn all the way to his shoulder. This may have its uses, but it is also used by horses who want to cheat and avoid the stretch you are asking for.

Step 2

Repeat the whole process from the top of the neck without allowing the horse to return each time you move your working hand. This should become an easy, simple bend to either left or right.

Supporting the Horse with Your Body

Smaller Horses

This method can be used if you can safely, and easily, reach over the top of the horse's neck. Facing the head, place your hip against the neck and reach over and hold the horse's face on either side. Using your hip as support to the neck, bring the head and neck round to the side, remembering to move your body to facilitate the turn.

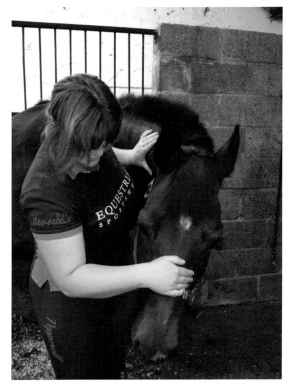

Side stretch towards you.

118

Side stretch on a smaller pony.

Larger Horses

This method will not work for very tall horses, or for smaller people, but instead of having the hands over the neck, come up from underneath and bend the horse around your supporting shoulder. It is necessary to keep the contact with the horse's neck with your shoulder as you turn, otherwise you will lose that support needed for the horse to bend around.

All of these techniques are designed to achieve the same thing, namely a correct bend to left and right, and so it does not matter which one you use. Try them all and find the ones that work best for you. Remember, however, that a technique may work for you with one horse but another method might be preferable for another horse. Always start with the side the horse finds it easier to bend and be aware that, sometimes, you might need to do a forward stretch before the side ones but for other horses, you might need side stretches before getting a good forward stretch. Making things as easy as possible for the horse gives us more chance of gaining his cooperation and therefore experiencing success.

Head Work

Head work is delicate, subtle and deeply effective. Not only do many channels end or begin on the head, but it is an area where many horses carry a lot of tension. Horse 'headaches' are not a recognisable veterinary term but given the tension that many horses hold in their heads and necks, I see no reason why a horse should not suffer from headaches in the same way as a human being. Certainly, when you look into their eyes, internal pain and discomfort is visible. The origin of that pain may very well be elsewhere but, as human beings are very much aware, even if your pain originates from somewhere else, if you have a bad headache, you do not care about that other pain. You want rid of the headache.

If your horse's head problem originates elsewhere, for instance, from an imbalance in the hind legs, then hopefully you will be able to help this with other work from this book. Often, however, if the headache is deep seated and has been carried around for some time, head work is very much required for the horse to believe and let go. There are no particular rules as to where on the head to start but, for now, we will start at the top and work down the face. When working on the head, it is very important not to put pressure on the halter; if you feel comfortable with the horse, either take the halter off completely or tie it around the neck. Whatever you do, it is vital that no downward pressure from the halter is caused while you are working, as this will generally defeat the object of the exercise.

The Poll

Poll tension is the result of many different possibilities, from problems in that area to ones that originate much further back. At the front end, you can have direct trauma, pull-back, ill-fitting bridles, neck misalignments and jaw tension. Problems with the hyoid apparatus and TMJ are one of the most common reasons for poll problems. The soft tissue structures in these areas are all connected and so an issue on any one of them will have a knock-on effect. After a while, this can result in tension in the shoulders as well for the same reason.

Step 1

Very gently lay your hand over the top of the neck, just behind the skull. You may feel a tight band on either or both sides where the brachiocephalicus meets the poll at its point of origin. This area should feel soft but if you can feel a band of tension then just let your fingers sit quietly until you feel it melt. Be patient and do not use any more pressure than the weight of your hand.

Step 2

Yes, Yes

With your hand over the poll so that your thumb sits just behind one side of the skull and your forefinger on the other, gently hold. With your other hand, hold the nasal bone and encourage the horse to nod, as if saying 'yes'. As the working hand nods the head, you should be able to feel any restriction in the hand that sits over the poll. It may be that there is a difference between one side and the other. Take a mental note of this as when you come to work on the ears, you will want to start on the more supple side.

No, No

Staying in the same position, this time, instead of the head moving up and down, the hand on the nose will move it from side to side, as if saying 'no'. It is just the lower half of the face that moves and the hand over the poll holds the head as if it was a pendulum. This part of the head will still be able to move but not as much and, once again, you should be able to feel any restrictions.

Stir the Porridge

Once again staying in the same position, this time you need to take the nose and ask it to turn circles in a slow, steady manner as if stirring something thick, like porridge.

These three techniques should be done one after the other as each one is progressively more difficult. However, it can work wonders for many tensions, including atlas/axis misalignments. If the horse finds any of this very difficult, or is concerned about it, then you might find that working somewhere else on the head first is a better place to begin.

The Ears

Many horses are sensitive around the ears and, again, there are many different reasons. There may be a problem with the ears themselves such as aural plaques. There may be tension in the many muscles around the base of the ear, which could be the result of ill-fitting tack, problems with the TMJ or misappropriate handling where the ear has

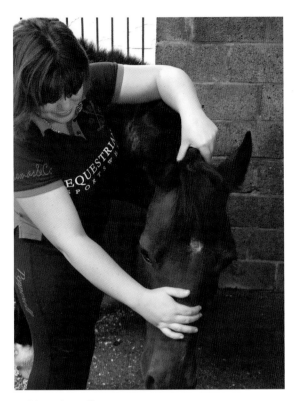

Holding the poll.

What's in the Name

When I started teaching in France, they wanted to give all the techniques different names so that they could identify them. Because I am Scottish and porridge is a traditional Scottish dish, 'Stir the Porridge' was born. Some of the names were a little more fanciful, including the technique mentioned in Chapter 8 where you move up into the 'armpit' at the top of the front leg. It was decided that this feeling of the skin moving upwards was like putting on a pair of stockings and so this technique became 'Les Chaussettes'.

been pulled or twitched. However, there is another possibility that is not so commonly thought about and that is a restriction further back in the body, such as the neck or even the back. If you want the ears to move forward, the skin and muscles of the neck and ultimately the back should move too but restriction, especially in the atlas/axis area of the neck, could result in this being uncomfortable or even painful. Issues such as this can lead to difficulties in putting on the halter or bridle. However, if the following techniques are applied, along with alleviating tension in the neck and back, often this can be resolved fairly quickly.

Holding the Head while You Work

There are two options for holding the head while you work; which you and the horse prefer is a matter of choice. For sensitive or large horses, option b) is probably easier and this is not just for the ears but for the rest of the face too.

Option a)

Stand facing the side of the horse's face and place one hand over his nasal bone. If you hold your hand too low, you could interfere with his breathing. The other hand will be the working hand. Be careful not to press down with the supporting hand as you will put pressure on the poll, jaw and also the nose.

Option b)

Stand beside the horse's head, facing forward, and wrap one hand up from under the jaw until the hand is holding the nasal bone. With this option, the horse does not feel so trapped and can raise his head up to move away, and it is easier to simply block this movement unless he is really unhappy about it. It is also the easier option if the horse is quite a lot taller than you or has a very high head carriage.

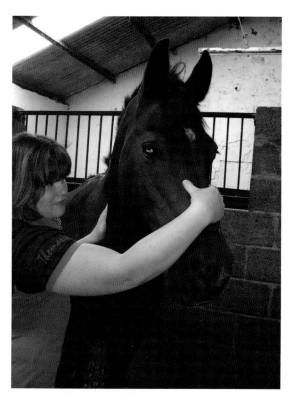

Option a) for working on the head.

Option b) for working on the head.

When Option a) or b) Will Not Work

There are some horses who really dislike being held using either method and here we have to improvise to get the job done. In this situation, place the supporting hand somewhere that the horse finds comfortable, such as halfway down the neck, or higher if possible, and then you can work with the other hand. This means that the head is unrestrained in any way so take care to avoid a potentially large, flying piece of bone, in other words, the head. If you bang heads with a horse, it hurts you more than him! What having to use this method tells us, however, is that there are definitely issues around the head that need dealing with to make the horse more comfortable.

Moving the Whole Ear

Holding the head with your preferred option, take your other hand and lay it flat against the side of the horse's head, just below the ear. Spread your fingers so that your forefinger is opened away from the other three fingers, creating a V shape that can surround the base of the ear. If the horse is happy with this, you can start at the base of the ear, but if he is not then begin lower and wider so that you do not touch the ear itself. Now move the skin in a circular motion, so that the ear begins to circle. If your horse is sensitive then it may take time before the ear itself can move but, gradually, he should begin to accept this and you can continue until it moves with ease.

Moving the ear.

Working Up the Sides of the Ear

Starting at the base of the ear, hold the edge of the ear between your forefinger and thumb. Squeeze gently and lift up a few millimetres, move the fingers up and repeat until you reach the tip of the ear. Repeat with the other edge of the ear. If you do not want to change hands, as this can sometimes upset the horse, use your thumb and the knuckle of your bent forefinger. To do all of this correctly, even tiny movements like this need to be done with body movement rather than just pulling the ears with your fingers.

Stretching the Ears

Holding the tip of the ear, stretch the ear forward, backward, up and out to the side. Once again, use you whole body to elicit the stretch. Sometimes you will find that you really need this as the horse reacts to enhance the stretch. It does not matter in

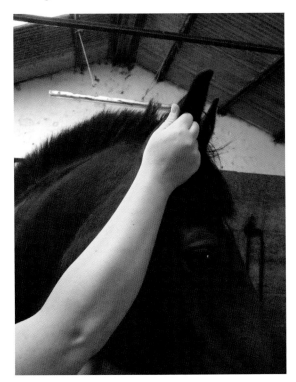

Up outside of the ear.

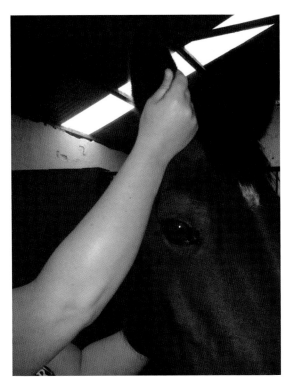

Up inside of the ear.

which order you do these stretches but it is worth noting which directions are easier or more difficult. When you have done this you can then massage the skin over the forehead and move down to either the cheeks or the eyes.

The Cheeks

The cheeks, and in particular, the masseter muscles, are not an area of the horse that is given much attention but horses that are tight in this area give the impression of sucking lemons. These muscles are part of the apparatus that is involved in the action of the jaw when chewing food and, as such, should be full and fleshy. Because of this, the cheeks lend themselves to the same technique as moving muscle over the hindquarters. From the edge of the lower jaw, push the muscle upwards with the heel of your hand, allowing the fat of the muscle to fill your palm. Gently work all around this area until it is released.

The Eyes

Working around the eyes is delicate, but can also be profound, due to the fact that several channels end, or begin, around the eyes. You can use either method of holding the head, but I prefer wrapping the supporting hand under and around the head, as this allows you to look directly into the horse's eyes as you work and you can see them soften and relax. Using the very tips of your fingers so that you do not poke them into the horse's eye, work along the lower eye socket from the inside corner to the outer one. Pressure still needs to be at 90 degrees and so this will be straight down, using body movement rather than pressing. If you have fingernails that are too long to do this safely then you can use the outer edge of your little finger.

For the upper eye socket, work from the outer corner to the inside one by placing your thumb on the underside of the socket and your forefinger directly above it, on the top of the eye socket; gently bring the forefinger to meet the thumb. Be patient and take your time with this work, as it is something that looks very simple but can be very relaxing and deeply effective. You can then massage down the tear ducts, thus clearing the channel down to the nostrils. It should feel like a hollow tube running down the face.

The Nostrils

There are also channels that finish at the nostrils, or pass nearby, but interestingly this is one of the areas where the horse can often prefer fast, vigorous work. Why this might be is not truly known. However, my theory is that because you are nearing the end of channels and there are a lot of nerve endings around the nose, as Ki moves, it feels like pins and needles and so needs rapid movement to stop the prickly sensation. Begin by rubbing over the nostrils with the flat of your hand to help alleviate this sort of feeling before the horse allows you to start more precise work. Start slowly and gently and build it up to a level preferred by your horse. Then you can begin to work the nostrils more precisely.

Whether you begin with the top side of the nostril or the underside is a matter of choice. Whatever you decide to use, start at the inside, as with the eye work, and take hold of the edge of the nostril between your forefinger and thumb; stretch it gently, curving outwards as if you were peeling an orange. You are not pulling the nostril straight out but rather easing it away from the centre. Work along the edge of the nostril until you reach the outside and then come back to the inside corner and repeat along the other side that still needs to be worked. Horses can find this technique rather strange until they realise what is happening and then usually really enjoy it.

The Mouth

Work on the mouth is useful for a variety of issues. Young horses that are teething will enjoy this work and horses that are constantly nibbling and chewing on items such as ropes and bits of your clothing are

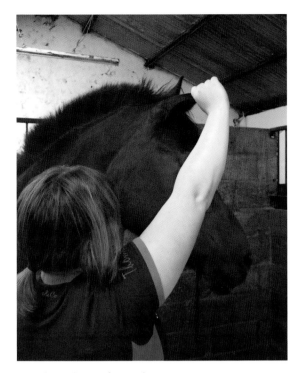

Stretching the ear forward.

Upward.

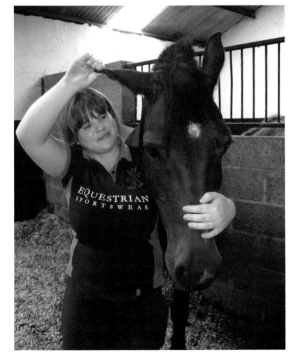

Outward.

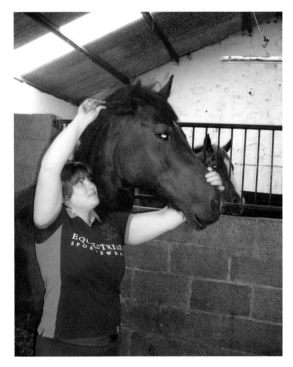

Backward.

Moving masseter muscle to release the cheeks.

often looking for some kind of satisfaction from the mouth and so this work can help to lessen these traits. They are unlikely to stop them altogether because it has become a habit and a comfort, but it can reduce both the amount and the intensity of the chewing.

Work on the mouth is also very beneficial for loosening off tension in the hyoid apparatus and the TMJ. There are some very simple, but very effective, techniques that can be used for this, one of which will be considered in the following text. When working inside the mouth, you obviously need to be careful of your fingers near the horse's teeth and so, while up until this point it has been best for the fingers to be relaxed, here it is better to keep them firmly together, taking care not to have one finger left out on its own. When working inside the mouth, it is preferable for the fingers to slide easily over the gums and bars, so if the horse has a dry mouth, it might be necessary to wet your hands first.

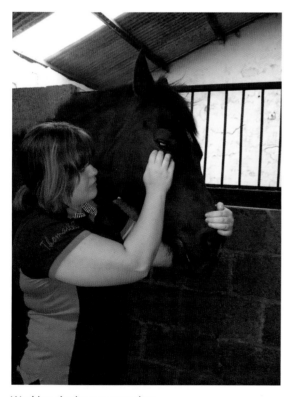

Working the lower eye socket.

Working the upper eye socket.

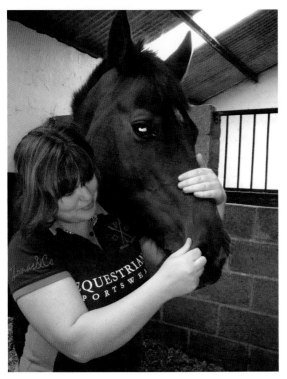

How to hold the nostril.

Stretching the nostril outwards.

Stretching the inside of the nostril.

The Upper Gum

Right in the middle of the upper gum, where the gum meets the lip, there is a little depression in the bone. This point is known as Governing Vessel 26 (GV 26) and it is a very powerful point for releasing built-up Ki in the head. In effect, it is one of the acupoints that acts like a turned-on tap to remove pressure on a dam and has much the same effect. This technique works better if you can support the horse's head with the arm coming under the jaw to hold the nose. This way, if the horse tosses his head up, you are more able to stay with him but also less likely to get smacked in the face by his head!

With your palm facing towards you, stretch out your thumb in the opposite direction to your fingers and keep the stretch taut. Slide your hand up the upper lip until you reach the top of the gums and then move your hand from side to side, back and forward along the gums. The horse may open his

The Compulsive Nibbler

One of the horses that lives with me has two damaged front teeth. The first one happened on the boat over from The Netherlands, when he was four years old. The second one occurred when he first arrived here as an eleven year old, as he tried to rearrange some windbreaks around the barn. He is now twenty-three and although he manages to eat quite easily, the teeth have definitely seen better days. The vets did not want to remove them because it would cause his bottom teeth to keep growing, without restriction. How much these teeth bother him is something we can only guess, but he is a compulsive nibbler – clothes, toggles, ropes, halters; if he cannot find anything, he likes to rubs his teeth backward and forward along the metal gates. It is therefore my opinion that he does feel discomfort and rubbing or moving his mouth helps to alleviate this and bring him some kind of satisfaction.

If we do the mouth techniques with him, this relief comes more quickly and he becomes less 'chewy' overall.

As an aside, this makes him a brilliant horse for Equine Shiatsu students to work with because, apart from anything else, he also considers this part of the game to see if he can annoy people. If someone is of the school of thought that all horses should stand quietly and not move while being worked on, and that horses are not allowed to express an opinion, then they get to work with this horse. As I have said many times previously, we work with the horse and adapting to a horse like this can be very difficult for some people. Because he sees it all as some sort of game, the more annoyed someone becomes, the more he keeps going; only by acknowledging the game but persuading him to go along with what you want to do will you gain any control of the situation.

mouth, move his jaws from side to side, raise or lower his head or even start to yawn. If this happens, just do your best to stay with him wherever he goes. Do not worry if none of these things happen, especially the first time, as many horses have never experienced someone rubbing their gums and they can appear quite confused to begin with.

After a few moments, move your fingers along until you find GV 26 and place the tip of your forefinger on top of it, taking care that your other fingers are clear of any teeth. For some horses, you can just rest your finger on the spot but for others, you might need to give it a little massage to get a response. The most common response is for the horse to stretch out his head and neck to reach into the pressure, so do not restrict your movement and be prepared to stretch your arm and whole body forward to allow a good head and neck stretch. You may find that if

the horse feels a restriction further back in his body, he starts to take a step forward; you can block this with your bottom, as mentioned in the forward neck stretch technique, because this is simply an extension of that, but now there is a stretch to the end of the nose.

The Lower Gum

This is exactly the same procedure except this time you are going to work on the lower gum and the acupoint in the middle is known as Conception Vessel 24 (CV 24). Slide your fingers, in the same position as mentioned previously, down to the bottom of the gum, slide from side to side and then use the forefinger to find the point in the middle of the gum just before it reaches the lips. Most horses show a

Working the upper gum.

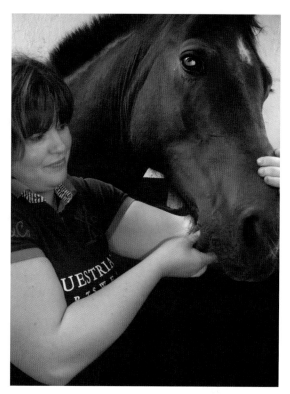

Working the lower gum.

stronger reaction to the upper-gum work and GV 26, but there are always some who prefer the lower-gum work.

Releasing the Hyoid Apparatus and TMJ

Tension in these areas can produce a huge variety of problems throughout the length of the horse's body. Apart from issues that relate directly to the head and neck, one of the next areas to show tightness is the shoulder, but if the initial source of tension is in the head then this must be addressed to solve any subsequent lack of movement through the shoulder. Likewise, problems found in the pelvis and SI joint can lead to tension in the head and, once again, it is necessary to consider the source. Attention also needs to be paid to tack fitting, and this includes saddles and martingales, as well as bridles and bits.

Just as there are many different reasons for tension in these areas, so there are many different techniques, and therapies, that can help alleviate that tension. However, this next technique is so simple and so effective that anyone can do it and thus help their horse to possibly great effect.

To release tension found on the right-hand side of the horse, you will need to work the left side of the mouth and vice versa. If your horse is unhappy with work around the ears or on top of the head, is reluctant to stretch out his jaw or is stiff in the shoulder, then this technique may be worth trying. If you can, hold the head as before. It is worth noting that some horses with tension here will not tolerate any restriction on the nose, as that itself can cause more tension in the area that is already tight and the horse knows that if his head is held in then it will hurt. It therefore may be necessary to put your supporting hand somewhere over the top of the neck, where the horse is comfortable. Slide two fingers onto the bars of the mouth and, if necessary, rub along them. The horse should begin to move his jaws from side to side. Note if he goes more to one side than the other or if just the bottom jaw is moving. He may yawn and move his head up and down, or over to one side or the other. Sometimes, he can move his head all over the place and you should just do your best to stay with him. All these things will help to release the TMJ and it is possible that he has already done this while using previous techniques, but ultimately what you are looking for is tongue movement.

Tongue movement is what releases the hyoid apparatus and to release tension on the right side of the head, the horse needs to stick his tongue all the way out to the left. I have several horses that can wrap their tongues around my wrist as I do this technique. However, to begin with, especially if they are tight here, then all you get is the tongue moving around in the mouth as they experiment with what they can do and feel. If your horse finds this difficult, you can accept the tip of the tongue reaching outside the lips. It means that he understands what is required and, left to his own devices, will probably work it out for himself. It is not unusual for horses to yawn and play about with their jaws for several minutes after you have finished. However, if they do not stop, you may have to help make the progress they are looking for by giving the bars another rub or even just holding your finger on them.

Releasing the Cheeks

This technique can be done one side at a time or both sides together. The latter is very satisfactory for both giver and receiver but for some horses it is too much for them to accept initially. It will stretch the cheeks downwards from the TMJ, which is not a movement that the horse will be used to and he is therefore unlikely to understand what you are asking of him, when you begin. It can also involve yawning at the same time and so, once again, you need to be very sure

of where your fingers – or in this case, thumbs – find themselves.

Two-Sided Technique

Stand directly in front of the horse and slide your thumbs up the sides of the mouth. Grasp the skin between your thumb and the rest of your fingers on each side. A fairly firm hold is required to prevent the hands slipping off. You can lift the edge of the horse's mouth out from the teeth to be sure that you are safe and secure. Then gently pull the cheeks downward, relax and repeat two or three times, if the horse accepts this stretch.

One-Sided Technique

For this method, you need to hold the horse's head as mentioned in previous techniques, with the arm coming up from under the jaw to hold the nose. You are, of course, standing behind the horse's head and then you can slide the thumb of your other hand up and under the side of the mouth, easing the skin outwards from the teeth. Grasp the skin between thumb and fingers and gently stretch down. To move from one side to the other, replace your hand over the horse's nose with the working hand and duck under his neck. You are then in position to work the other side without losing connection between you and the horse.

All of this work on the mouth is very beneficial to so many horses. A horse that is unhappy in his mouth can create tension that runs the full length of his body and so this work can have a huge effect on how the horse feels about himself, and his way of going. However, all this movement of Ki in and around the head can leave the horse appearing as if he is light-headed or very sleepy. We therefore want to move that Ki and his consciousness away from the head. The simplest way to do this is to work on the tail.

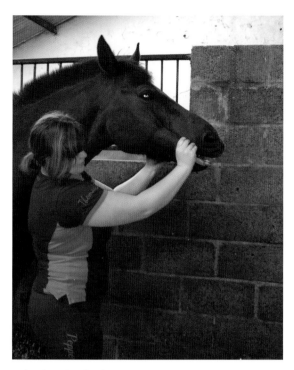

Releasing the cheeks.

Work on the Tail

The tail is more than a fly swatter or for use as a warning signal. It is part of the spine and, as such, it needs to be free and flexible. Of course, some horses clamp their tails as soon as you touch them and this can be for a variety of reasons; even so, we need the horse to be happy and willing to have his tail handled as well as it being able to swing without tension. You should be able to flick the tail as if you were lifting it for the fillet string of a rug. If the horse cannot do this, or is unhappy or tense while trying it, then there is a problem of some kind, somewhere.

Before we move on to specific techniques for the tail, perhaps it would be useful to look at a simple solution to aiding the spine to relax and allow the tail to move more easily. On the midline of the spine, you might find two depressions. One will be just in front of the sacroiliac joint and the other will be about halfway down the sacrum.

Position to relax the tail.

Test the ability and fluidity of the tail to lift. It does not need to be high – to the horizontal is more than enough. Then place a hand in both depressions until you feel warmth. If your horse lowers his head and begins to relax, you may want to wait a little longer. You can then test the tail movement again. It may not be perfect but, hopefully, there will be some improvement and you can do this every day to keep it going. If you have a horse with kissing spines that can be ridden, this is an excellent way to see how he is feeling on the day you want to ride.

The coccygeal vertebrae can also be considered as a mirror of the cervical vertebrae. The top of the tail corresponds with the bottom of the neck, and the end of the tail with the atlas/axis. Misalignments felt in the tail will match with those in the neck and so if you have a horse that is really uncomfortable with you working on his neck, you may be able to work on his tail instead.

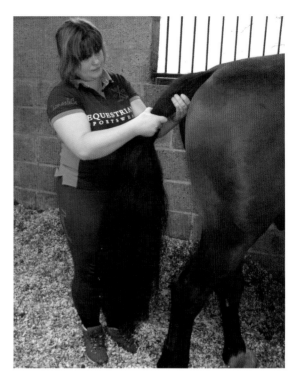

Rotating the tail.

Tail Rotations

Standing directly behind the horse, pick up the top of the tail in one hand and stroke down the underside of the dock with one hand and then the other to encourage the horse to relax. Hold the top of the tail in one hand, with the other hand holding just underneath. Keeping the uppermost hand still, rotate the other hand on a horizontal plane. Ideally this should, as always, be done with body movement so that your hips will rotate, as if using a hula hoop, and your arm and hand will follow to create the rotation. Rotate two or three times and then move the rotating hand down a few centimetres and repeat. Continue down until you reach the bottom of the tail, taking note of any areas of tension or restriction and see if they correspond to the neck or not.

Incremental Stretches

Lift the tail up, but without going above the horizontal; this time, you are going to stretch out sections of

the tail at a time. It is not an attempt to stretch every single vertebrae individually but rather in small groups. Holding the tail at the top, lean back to create a stretch while carefully observing the horse's ears for his reaction. With the other hand, push the rest of the tail away from you to enhance the stretch of that particular part. Keeping the supporting hand at the top of the tail, bring the other hand down a few centimetres and repeat. Continue in this way until you reach the bottom of the tail.

Side Stretches

When asking for a stretch to the side with the tail, it is not just the tail that will be stretched. You should be able to feel the stretch reach to the pelvis and the ribs. If your horse goes for this stretch in a big way, be prepared to hold on tight and use your whole body weight to counterbalance the horse. Sometimes they

Incremental stretches.

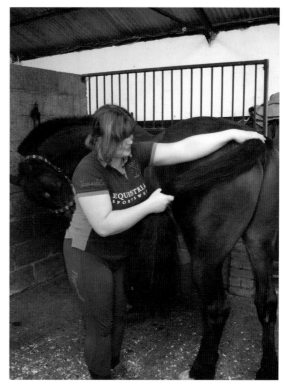

Side tail stretch .

can lean right over and for this and for the full spinal stretch, you need to be careful how you come out of the stretch so that the horse knows that he has to regain his balance.

Standing at the side of the horse, grasp the top of the tail from above and lower down the dock with the other hand; lean back until you meet a point of resistance and wait until the horse understands what is going on and leans away from you to enhance the stretch. Try to meet his amount of stretch with an equal amount from you and do not simply pull. The more the horse puts into the stretch, the more weight you need to counteract him and so remember to use your whole body and not just pull with your arms.

To move to the other side, gradually release the stretch until you and the horse are upright and there is no pressure left. Without letting go of the tail, begin to move around to the other side, allowing the hand at

the top of the tail to slide down to nearer the bottom of the dock; as you move into position on the other side, grasp the top of the tail with your other hand and then repeat the procedure. You can then come back to centre, behind the horse, to give a full spinal stretch.

Full Spinal Stretch

In general, horses love this and can stretch their heads and necks right out in a horizontal line. This makes it a very satisfying technique to end a session and will leave the horse feeling totally relaxed. However, it is not obligatory to wait until the end of the session if you feel that the horse needs to feel how to stretch his topline during his Shiatsu. For example, if your horse has struggled with the wither stretch, mentioned at the beginning of this chapter, then it might help him to achieve this if you stretch his tail beforehand.

Rather than just go directly into a full stretch, it is better to try a pull-and-relax approach first. As well as preparing the horse for what is about to happen, it also allows you to see if the back muscles are able to extend and relax evenly on both sides, and reach the whole length of the back. If the horse finds this difficult, instead of give and take of the muscles, you will find that he sways his whole body and thus avoids using the muscles. If your horse has had a very tight back but you have successfully loosened it off, the pull-and-relax method will gently show him that things can now move.

So, holding the tail about halfway down the dock, lean back to a point of tension, hold for a few moments and come back up, allowing the muscles to relax. Repeat several times until you see, or feel, the muscles moving. If your horse is very large and you cannot see his back, then a helper can look for you. As you repeat the pull-and-relax, the horse should begin to understand what is being asked of him and will begin to stretch away from you. You can then go for the big, final stretch and lean your body weight backwards, while the horse leans forward. Hold until the horse comes back out of the stretch, or for as long as you can – with some horses you could be there for some time! Once again, you need to release slowly so that the horse does not fall forward. Maintain the amount of stretch as you bring yourself to an upright position, and then very gradually start to let go so the horse becomes responsible for his own balance. Only once he is fully standing with his weight on all four legs should you let go by sweeping down the length of the tail.

The Finish

In the same way as there was a body sweep at the beginning of the Shiatsu session, so there needs to be something to say 'the end' to give a feeling of completion. There are a variety of different ways of doing

Full spinal stretch.

this and it is simply a matter of what you and your horse prefer.

Option 1: Bl Sweep

If the horse is not too large, you can reach over the withers so that you have a hand on either side of the back, on the Bladder channel, and simply sweep along the back, over the hindquarters and away. This will give an energetic connection but also a feeling of closing down and an end to the session.

Option 2: Connecting through the Spine

There is a channel, known as Governing Vessel, that runs along the topline of the horse, over the top of the dorsal spinous processes. It is not actually a channel like the Bladder channel but is considered to be a reservoir of Ki, which the body can use to add or store Ki, in the same way as a reservoir uses water.

With this technique, there are different points that you could place your hands:

a) One hand at the top of the withers, the other in front of the sacroiliac joint
b) One hand in front of the sacroiliac joint, the other halfway down the sacrum
c) One hand on the lowest part of the back, the other wherever your instinct tells you

Place both hands over your chosen areas and wait until the horse starts to relax. Allow him to accept and enjoy the process, so do not rush him. When you feel that you have waited long enough, let your hands get lighter and lighter, until they gently float upwards and off the body. Step away from the horse and give him a moment to process things. Some horses do not take long over this but others will appear to fall asleep, while some move areas of their body to feel, and assess the changes. If possible, turn your horse out so that he can move about and work out what has changed. If this is not possible, an alternative is to take him for a short walk.

CHAPTER 11

The Final Touches

Let the Magic Begin

Equine Shiatsu is a truly magical therapy and can achieve the most amazing results, even for a complete beginner. However, it does turn the general accepted way of deciding what to do in any given circumstance on its head. For most people, the idea is that you learn theory and practice first in order to know what to do with each particular situation and, not only that, but that the same protocol can be used in any similar cases. Among other things, this also makes it easier to prove significantly if something works or not. It is not that there is little theory behind Shiatsu (in fact, quite the opposite) but it is accepted that every being is an individual, and as such, can manifest similar symptoms for many differing reasons. Learning to trust what you feel and what the horse is telling you, and indeed, learning from the horse, is the first step in this great journey. Working on every different horse offers a unique experience and can still, after over twenty years, continue to surprise and amaze. There are no rules, only guidelines, and observation and quality of touch are key to good Shiatsu, using the tools described in this book.

Listen to Your Hands

Some horses can relax within seconds of the initial touch, but not all. While it is gratifying, and for a beginner, reassuring, when the horse develops that sleepy eye, drops the head and neck, sighs loudly or begins to yawn, it is what is happening under your hands that is more important. Feeling the muscles soften, the joints wiggle more easily and life seeming to return, as the warmth and movement appear under your palms or fingers as the fascia unwinds, is ultimately what you are looking for. Be patient, expect nothing and remember to breathe. Do not worry if the horse does not show outward signs of relaxation because as long as the body that you are touching is responding, you can be assured that all is well. In such cases, it can often be that once the horse is left on his own, he will let go mentally, as well as physically, and sleep.

Believing in the Concept of Ki

The theory behind Shiatsu is completely logical if you can accept the presence of Ki but sometimes there is confusion in that Ki is something different. A tight muscle or a stiff joint are just examples of imbalanced Ki. Ascertaining whether the imbalance is excessive or deficient Ki comes with practice through touch. You can also consider what you know and see. For example, if you have a muscle in spasm, it may feel tight and while tightness can be a symptom of excessive Ki, where a muscle is in spasm because the blood supply is restricted, it means that there is not enough blood and so it is a deficient situation. The tension commonly occurs at the point of origin, point of insertion or both, and when this has been released, the blood supply can be restored. Whether this is described in this way or as a blockage in Ki that is released makes no difference – balance is restored, which is what matters.

Wow Moments

The objective is to cause a change within the horse for the better. Sometimes, this can be a small change initially but, likewise, it can sometimes be a massive one. A lot of this will depend on the receptiveness of the horse to accept change. However,

you should be able to see a positive result from the beginning, although at the start, you may find that two or three sessions are needed to feel that you are on the right track. If you are fortunate enough to get a huge change from the beginning, it may be tempting to ask, 'Did I do that?' The answer is that you allowed the horse to do it for himself. However, it is always a fabulous feeling to get a 'wow moment' as it shows you what a powerful therapy Equine Shiatsu can be. Ultimately, Shiatsu is a preventative therapy and regular sessions can transform any horse. Many of the elderly horses that I have worked with for many years now look better, and move better, than they did more than ten years ago. Most of them are still in work and some are also still competing.

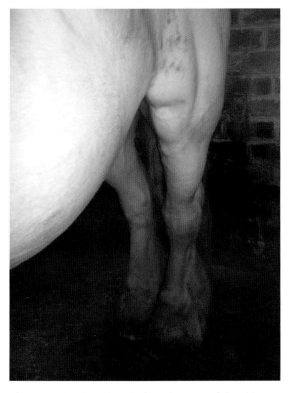

Close together hind legs before the start of the Shiatsu session.

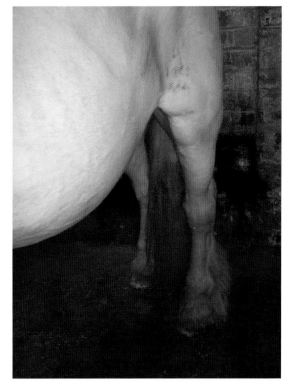

Evidence of change in the horse's stance after thirty minutes of Shiatsu.

Filius, ex 4* eventer, aged twenty-eight and still ridden.

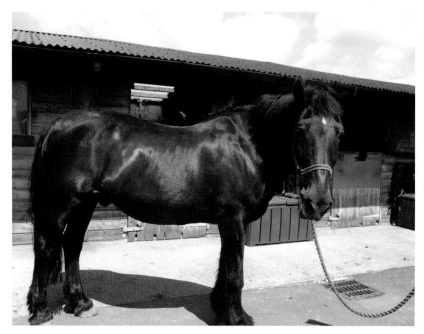

Rascal, aged twenty-six and still ridden.

Clancy, aged twenty-three, not ridden but still sound, despite having had stifle issues for ten years.

William, aged twenty-six, not ridden due to a heart problem, but still sound.

Rocky, aged twenty-eight and still ridden.

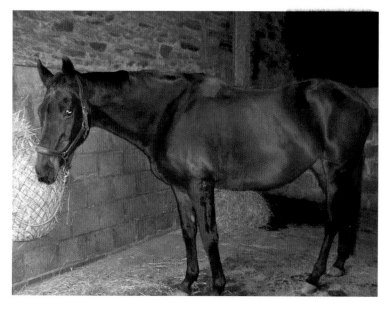

Ruby, aged twenty-three, ex-racer and still ridden.

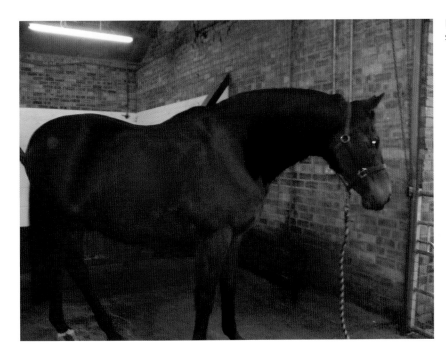

Elvis, aged twenty-three and still ridden.

Shiatsu for All

Equine Shiatsu is a wonderful therapy and whether it is used for fine-tuning of the fit and healthy horse, the maintenance and improvement of a horse with an existing condition, or as a general preventative medicine as it was originally intended, all horses can benefit.

Of course, horses are not the only animals who enjoy Shiatsu…

Charlie Brown enjoying a hind leg stretch. He was born with a deformed front leg but was sound until the day he died aged nineteen.

William can now jump and climb as he used to with regular Shiatsu.

Bibliography

Hedley, G., 'Fascia and Stretching: The Fuzz Speech' [video], YouTube (8 Feb. 2009), http://youtube.com/watch?v=_FtSP-tkSug, accessed 1 Dec. 2022

Keown, D., *The Spark in the Machine: How the Science of Acupuncture Explains the Mysteries of Western Medicine* (London: Signing Dragon, 2014)

Schultz, R.M., Due, T., and Elbrønd, V.S., *Equine Myofascial Kinetic Lines* (Kalmar: Lenanders Grafiska, 2021)

Index